A World of Books:
An Annotated Reading List
For ESL/EFL Students

Second Edition, Revised

A World of Books:
An Annotated Reading List
For ESL/EFL Students

Dorothy S. Brown

Berea College, Retired
Berea, Kentucky

Teachers of English to Speakers of Other Languages

Staff Editor: Juana E. Hopkins

Copyright © 1988 by
Teachers of English to Speakers of Other Languages
Washington, DC
Printed in the USA

Copying or further publication of the contents of this work is not permitted without permission of TESOL, except for limited "fair use" for educational, scholarly and similar purposes as authorized by the US Copyright Law, in which case appropriate notice of the source of the work should be given.

Library of Congress Catalog No. 87-051268
ISBN 0-939791-32-3

Table of Contents

A Word to Students 1

To the Teacher 3

Acknowledgements 10

A Note on the Bibliographic Data 11

Fiction 13

Nonfiction 39

Appendices 59
    I. Cross Reference: Location 61
    II. Cross Reference: Topics and *Genres* (Literary Types) 65
    III. Some Short and Easy Books 69
    IV. For Advanced Readers 70

For

Ruth Crymes
1924-1979

A Word to Students

An excellent way to increase your ability to use a language is to read extensively in it. If you enjoy reading in your native language, you already know what pleasure this activity can bring. But even if you are not an avid reader in another language, you may perhaps become one in English. There is certainly enough material available, in newspapers, magazines, and books.

This availability of materials is one of the problems. Millions of books have been written in English. The purpose of this annotated list is to help you find some that will interest you. Each selection is described in order to give you an idea of the subject. In addition, some are marked *Y*, if suitable for younger readers (as well as older ones, as a rule) and some are marked *M*, if more suitable for mature adults than for young people. You may also be helped by the appendices, in which the books listed are classified according to setting, subject matter, and level of difficulty.

You are the final judge, however, of whether or not a book will hold your interest. The 18th-century English essayist Francis Bacon wrote:

> Some books are to be tasted, others to be swallowed, and some few to be chewed and digested; that is, some books are to be read only in parts; others to be read but not curiously, and some few to be read wholly, and with diligence and attention.

In using this list you may need to "taste" several books before you find one that you wish to "swallow" or perhaps even to read "with diligence and attention."

Begin by selecting a few titles which appeal to you. Then go to your library and see which books are available. Check out several and take them home or to your dormitory room. Read a few pages, perhaps 10 or 20. If you find the reading uninteresting or difficult, or both, "taste" another book. Keep tasting until you find something of interest.

Many of the books listed are available in bookstores, in inexpensive paperback editions. You may want to buy some of them and start your own English language library.

While reading, do not worry if you do not recognize every word; often the meaning will be apparent because of the context. You may want to write down words that are unfamiliar. After you have finished reading a few pages or a chapter you can glance back to see if the meanings of these words have become clear. If not, *then* look them up in a dictionary, preferably a monolingual English dictionary. Be sure that the definition fits the word as it is used in the sentence or passage, for many words have more than one meaning.

The books in this list vary in difficulty, and you may want to begin with some of the short and easy ones listed in Appendix III. Remember, however, that a short book or a book which someone else considers easy may be difficult for someone who is unfamiliar with the subject or the setting. Every person's background, in language and in other aspects of culture as well, is unique. Since you know more about your ability to use English and about your cultural background than anyone else does, you are best able to decide, after "tasting" a book, whether or not you will enjoy reading it carefully.

To the Teacher

One purpose of this selected reading list is to help advanced ESL/EFL students and other nonnative speakers of English *who have attained a certain proficiency* to select suitable reading material. Another purpose is to suggest books which can be read by an entire class, though not all the books listed are appropriate for that purpose. Some, for example, are unavailable in paperback, and a few are translations from other languages.

In deciding when students should be encouraged to read books which have not been specially edited for their benefit, the classification of reading proficiency levels devised by the U.S. Foreign Service Institute may be useful. Here is the gist of this classification:

> *R-1—Elementary Proficiency.* At this stage, a person can read only the simplest prose containing the most common words and grammatical constructions. Heavy reliance on a dictionary is normal.
>
> *R-2—Limited Working Proficiency.* At this stage, a person can read uncomplicated but authentic prose that treats familiar topics and contains many common words and familiar sentence patterns. Frequent use of the dictionary is necessary.
>
> *R-3—Professional Proficiency.* At this level, a person can grasp the essentials of standard but uncomplicated prose . . . without a dictionary.
>
> *R-4—Full Proficiency.* At this level, [students] can read anything published in the foreign language without a dictionary. (Language learners are reminded that if they want to be able to read quickly and effortlessly in a foreign language, they must read as much in one as in the other).[1]

Most of the books listed in this bibliography are suitable for students who might be classified at the *R-3* level, though some can be read by students who would be classified as *R-2* and a few can be read with ease *only* by those in the *R-4* category. All the books have been selected with the following criteria in mind:

1. With occasional exceptions, the books do not exceed 300 pages. Most readers, especially those with less than full proficiency, are intimidated by length. A student who is prepared to read *Gone With the Wind* does not need guidance in selecting reading material.

2. They contain little or no nonstandard English, jargon, patois, or pidgin. Unless students have lived for a fairly long time in the community where such language is used (and it differs from one English-speaking country to another and even within the same country) they will be unnecessarily confused and often unable to get help from a dictionary. Even readers from other countries who speak English as well as they speak their native language will find *Huckleberry Finn* formidable, and most native speakers of English have trouble with *Uncle Remus*.

3. They contain nothing offensive to any race or group of people. This does not mean that no character in a book may express such opinions, but the author's point of view must be not only tolerant, but also appreciative, of the values and customs of all cultures.

4. They have all been written in the 20th century; most of them, in fact, have been written after 1945. Language changes with time, and books written in earlier centuries are usually best read in a literature class with the guidance of a teacher who can explain the customs, both linguistic and social, of the time.

5. They must be interesting. Not every book will interest every reader, but it is hoped that every book will appeal to a fairly large number of readers.

Somewhat hesitantly, I have listed what I consider the easiest books included in the bibliography. (See Appendix III.) This was a presumptuous undertaking; as far as I know there is no scientific method for evaluating the ease with which a book can be read by nonnative speakers, and I have relied to a great extent on instinct. I considered the length of the book (most are under 200 pages), the vocabulary and sentence length, and sometimes the age or grade level as given in *Books in Print*. The grade level, however, is not very reliable for our purposes, as it pertains to the reading level of native speakers rather than the reader's knowledge of the English language. It also differs among publishers, sometimes depending on the size of print or the type of illustrations in an edition.

Appendix IV lists books which are difficult and probably should be attempted only by readers of full proficiency. There are relatively few such books included in this bibliography.

Readers vary in age as well as in ability, so a wide range of material has been included. Some books will appeal especially to junior high students, some to high school students, some to undergraduate and graduage college students, and some, perhaps, to all of these groups. Entries that seem most suitable for younger readers are marked with a *Y*, but can often be read with pleasure by older readers as well. Books marked *M* are those which presuppose a certain familiarity with the subject of the book (politics, history, or science, for example) or which deal with social problems of little interest to younger readers. If listings are marked neither with *Y* nor *M* they are perhaps most appropriate for high school students and/or undergraduate college students, though many of them can be read by younger students as well. Although frequently books that are listed as "easy" will also be considered suitable for younger readers, this is not always the case. Rumer Godden's *The River*, though short and easy to read, would probably appeal more to college readers than to those in high school or junior high.

Since interest in and ability to understand a book depends not only on age and English reading proficiency but also on the reader's cultural background and intellectual interests, an effort has been made to include books on many subjects and set in many parts of the world. (See Appendices I and II.) Relevant background knowledge has been found to be a significant factor in reading comprehension, perhaps more important than language level.[2] Students of science will be able to read a biography of a scientist, a book on astronomy or space exploration, or even a science fiction novel with greater understanding than readers without such background. I have also found that students bring an added dimension to their reading of books about their native country and frequently read such books with a depth of understanding that surpasses my own. Since students of English as a second or foreign language are also interested in reading about the countries in which that language is used, many books set in English-speaking countries have been included.

After the nucleus of this list (fiction only) was distributed at the

1978 TESOL Convention in Mexico City, where I presented a paper titled "An Annotated Bibliography of Fiction for ESL Students," I was pleasantly surprised by the many requests for copies from teachers who had not been able to attend the convention. Later, especially after the publication of the first edition of the list (Austin, TX, 1979), I received many letters describing the ways in which it was being used. Many teachers welcomed it as a reference to paperback novels which could be read by an entire class. Several mentioned setting up a library, a browsing room, or a reading room for ESL/EFL students and wrote me that they had found the list useful in making selections.

A teacher of composition in the English for the Foreign Born Program at Queens College, New York requested the bibliography because many of her students had asked for a list of books that would help them develop their reading skills in English. A teacher at the University of Tennessee said that she had had requests from students for suggestions about books they could read.

An English teacher in Portugal reported that the list would be of interest not only to him but also to one of his assistants who was teaching a course called "Practical English." Another teacher in the Portuguese Azores felt that the bibliography would be useful both to him and to his students, who were either teachers or potential teachers of English.

Teachers in Sweden have used the bibliography in selecting books for class reading and assignments, for suggesting independent reading, and for helping students select books to read during vacations.

Virginia French Allen mentioned the possibility of using the bibliography for selecting books to be read by "peer partners," one of whom is a native speaker of English. This approach is probably most effective in secondary schools. As I understand it, two students, one a native speaker and one for whom English is not a native language, read the same book and discuss it with each other. Individual reports could include personal reactions to the book and a comment on the discussion with the peer partner.

In my own classes I have required each student to read one selection from the list each semester and to write a brief paper discussing it. Their reactions to the books selected have all been positive, perhaps because they were encouraged to select books on topics with which they were familiar and because the less proficient students were encouraged to read short and easy books. Their comments on the books have been of great interest to me, especially when they have brought first-hand knowledge of a book's setting to their evaluation, as did a young man from Bangladesh who wrote of a novel by Kamala Markandaya:

> ...I may have spent over twenty years of my life in the culture of Rukmani, the narrator of the story, but I never realized the unpredictability and the severity of the sufferings of the simple and innocent village folks like Rukmani, her peasant husband Nathan, or their daughter Irawaddy—all slaves of poverty... This is not just a story of Rukmani's fate, but is the truth about every poor home in Indian villages. This is what makes the book unique. It speaks for all of them. I have never felt so close to home since I have been here as I did while reading *Nectar in a Sieve*.

A student from Nigeria wrote the following critique of *Second-Class Citizen*, by Buchi Emecheta:

> ...Emecheta begins by setting the novel in a popular street in Yaba, one of the best areas in the capital city of Nigeria. Then she picks *Obi*, a common name amongst the Ibos, without apologizing to people whose names and background may fit into this setting. This fact is important, because I intend to show the difference between publishing in Nigeria for Nigerian readers and publishing for foreign readers. *Second-Class Citizen* is definitely for foreigners to read, and this perhaps explains why it has up till now not been published in Nigeria.... The title of the book itself, which urged me in the first place to read it, is highly controversial in Nigeria. After the civil war in the eastern part of the country in 1970, the Ibos in the war-affected region were apt to regard themselves as second-class citizens, having been brought back by force to "One Nigeria."

A student from Ghana interprets the same title as referring to the position of the women in Nigeria, since the main character is a woman, and objects to what he considers the author's theme:

> Although I come from basically the same cultural background as Adah and Francis, I find most of the incidents very hard to believe... most of Africa is growing out of the tendency to look down upon the woman as a second-class citizen.... Africa is presently abandoning many of the customs described in the novel. Marriages between Africans and Whites are very much tolerated these days; people don't bother too much about paying bride prices; and the white man is no longer looked upon as a semi-god. It is

important for all those who read this book to realize that the Africa the author talks about is the Africa of yesterday. The Africa of today is much more liberal and very different.

Other comments by students reflect their interest in reading and, perhaps more important, their ability to read on their own. The following excerpts have been edited by me and rewritten (in most cases, more than once) by the student writers. They do not, therefore, reflect the students' ability to write correctly. They do show, however, that ESL/EFL students can read with understanding and appreciation if the reading material is suitable.

A Korean student who had lived many years in Japan ended his discussion of Gwen Terasaki's book with this comment:

> *Bridge to the Sun* is a record of World War II reflected in the eyes of an American woman who survived the war and suffered with the people in Japan. The book shows that no actual hostilities among the peoples existed during the war. The political conflicts and ill considerations of a few malicious leaders brought about the brutal and unnecessary war.

A business major from Hong Kong wrote of Hemingway's *Old Man and the Sea:*

> I enjoyed reading the book because of its excellent descriptions of the loneliness and endurance of the old fisherman.

Most of my students were proficient in oral English and were able to do well in math and science classes. Their written English, however, often bewildered their teachers, and frequently they had trouble reading textbooks in courses such as history and psychology. But even those of lesser proficiency managed to read one book from our list and to comment intelligently on it. A young woman from China, a very bright physics major whose English was almost nonexistent when she arrived at Berea College, read Sheila Burnford's *Incredible Journey* and drew an interesting moral conclusion from the behavior of the main characters, two dogs and a cat:

> I love the story, but I love the trio much more, because I think we can learn something from them. We are human, but wars exist in the world and sometimes even fights occur in families. We are more intelligent than the animals are, but sometimes we cannot keep our goals firmly, and we lose them. I saw a moral in their characters: "Unless you

persevere with a subject you can't hope to master it." I would like to have friends who can keep the same relationship with me as the members of the trio kept to each other. We should help each other to go on our way to our final objective. The world is big; I believe that I can find such kind friends.

I enjoyed reading my students' reactions to the books they read, and I believe that they enjoyed reading the books and expressing their opinions about them. Resourceful teachers will no doubt be able to think of many other ways in which this bibliography can be used. Its main purpose, however, is simply to help students who are fairly proficient in English, but not completely at home in the cultures of English-speaking countries, to find books that they can read with a maximum of pleasure and a minimum of frustration.

Dorothy S. Brown

[1]Joan Rubin & Irene Thompson, *How to be a More Successful Language Learner.* Boston: Heinle & Heinle, 1982, pp. 28-30.

[2]Martin G. Levine and George J. Hause. "The Effect of Background Knowledge on the Reading Comprehension of Second Language Learners." *Foreign Language Annals, 18* pp. 391-397.

Acknowledgements

Compiling this bibliography would have been much more difficult and less rewarding without the help of others. I would like to express my appreciation to the following people who have given me help and encouragement:

The librarians in the Berea College Library, especially Edith Hanson, who ordered countless books for me through interlibrary loan; and Mary Hawley, Catherine Roberts, and Phyllis Hughes, who helped me track down elusive bibliographic data.

Charles H. Blatchford, who as Chair of the 1978 TESOL Convention accepted my proposal which led to the compiling of the first edition of this bibliography and who has encouraged me in writing this revised edition.

Members of the TESOL Publications Committee, who have offered me valuable advice as I worked on this edition, and especially Douglas Brown (Publications Chair, 1985), who answered my many inquiries with unrelenting patience.

Ron Eckard, editor of the *Kentucky TESOL Newsletter* (1979-1983), and Alice Osman, editor of the *TESOL Newsletter* (1982-1987), who published my article, "Selecting Books for ESL/EFL Students" in their respective newsletters.

Teachers who took the time to send suggestions as requested in that article, especially Nancy Hottel-Burkhart, Texas A & M University; Ann Silverman, University of Pennsylvania; Carol Lazzeri, University of Miami; and Judy Gex, LaGuardia Community College, New York City.

Bobby Fong, Berea College Department of English, who introduced me to some excellent Chinese-American authors, and Elise André, Berea College Foreign Language Department, who shared her expertise in language learning and supplied me with valuable material on reading in a foreign language.

Elisabet Lindqvist, English teacher in Gothenburg, Sweden, who told me about books by American authors that her students enjoy reading.

Teachers who wrote to me after the distribution of the original list in Mexico or after the publication of the first edition and suggested books or described the ways in which they found the list useful, especially Winifred Falcon, Columbia University; Bob Pesek, University of Toledo; Virginia French Allen, Boulder, Colorado; Edward S. Franchuk, Instituto Universitário dos Açores, Portugal; and Marcia

Reznik, Queens College, New York.

Teachers who read the completed manuscript and helped me make final decisions: Winifred Falcon, Judy Gex, Elisabet Lindqvist, and Carol Lazzeri. I adopted many of their suggestions, but since I had to make the final decisions I remain responsible for the faults and shortcomings of this list.

D.B.

A Note on Bibliographic Data

The bibliographic data was obtained by consulting *Books in Print, British Books in Print, Canadian Books in Print,* and *Indian Books in Print;* by examining the title pages of the books themselves; and sometimes by writing letters of inquiry to publishers.

If a book is out of print entirely, *(op)* precedes the entire entry. If a cited edition is out of print, *(op)* appears after the place of publication. Reprint editions are listed only if they are the only hard cover editions still in print. Editions published in England, Canada, and occasionally in other countries are included for the convenience of instructors teaching outside the United States. Such information may be incomplete, however, and it is advisable to place orders, whenever possible, through a local book dealer.

Very few of the listings are completely out of print—one fiction and a half-dozen nonfiction. These books are available in libraries and in second-hand bookstores.

The date listed for each entry is the copyright date, which appears immediately after the author's name and the title. In the case of translations, the original date of publication is in parentheses. Wherever possible, the page count is given for the first hard cover edition. If the page count was unavailable for that edition, it is given for a later (often paperback) edition.

Fiction

Achebe, Chinua. *Things Fall Apart: The Story of a Strong Man.* (1960). London: Heinemann. 215 pp.

Available in paperback from Heinemann, London; Astor-Honor, New York; Fawcett, New York.

The central character of this novel set in Nigeria is Okonkwo. He is a hard-working farmer, a domineering husband, and a strict father. He accidentally kills a fellow clansman and is banished to the home of his mother's kinsmen. When he returns to his own home, he finds that during his absence missionaries have arrived, the British government is replacing tribal customs, and the strong ties of kinship in the community have weakened. This novel shows the strengths and weaknesses of a primitive society and the effects on it, both good and bad, of western civilization.

A sequel, *No Longer at Ease*, depicts the sometimes tragic consequences of rapid cultural change in a developing country. The main character is the grandson of Okonkwo.

Adams, Douglas. *The Hitchhiker's Guide to the Galaxy.* (1979). New York: Crown. 215 pp.

Available in paperback from Pocket, New York; Pan, London.

The best word to describe this book is *zany*, which means both strange and comic. Arthur Dent lies down in front of a bulldozer to prevent it from destroying his house so that a new road can be built. Later, about 12 minutes before the end of Earth, Arthur's friend Ford Prefect persuades Arthur to get up and go with him to a pub, where they order drinks. While they are drinking, a voice from a ship in outer space announces that Earth must be demolished so that an express route through the star system can be built. Still later, traveling on a space ship, Arthur and Ford have many exciting adventures.
M

Aldrich, Bess Streeter. *A Lantern in Her Hand.* (1928). New York: D. Appleton. (op)

Reprint edition available from Amereon, New York. Available in paperback from New American Library, New York. 251 pp.

Abbie Mackenzie refuses the proposal of a young man who wants to take her east to New York, where she could develop her talents in art or music. Instead, she marries Will Deal, who takes her west to Nebraska, which in the 1870s is undeveloped territory. There Abbie and Will raise a large family and help build a new community, and Abbie eventually sees her dreams fulfilled by her children and grandchildren.

This novel describes life in a midwestern prairie state when it was first being settled.

Anaya, Rudolfo. *Bless Me, Ultima.* (1972).

Available in paperback from Tonatiuh International, Berkeley, CA. 248 pp.

Antonio, a 7-year-old Mexican Indian boy, narrates this novel which is filled with excitement, suspense, and fear of the supernatural. His father's people and his older brothers are *vaqueros* (cowboys), and his mother's relatives are farmers. Antonio's desire to become a farmer-priest leads him to explore the world of Ultima, who blends her Christian faith with Indian folklore. Antonio tries to reconcile the teachings of the Church with Ultima's faith and also with a young friend's belief in the powers of a beautiful large fish.

Bradbury, Ray. *Fahrenheit 451.* (1953). New York and Toronto: Random House. (op).

Available in paperback from Ballantine Books, New York; Random House of Canada, Toronto; Fitzhenry & Whiteside, Markham, Ontario; Panther, London. 184 pp.

This science fiction story is about the censorship of books. The protagonist, Guy Montag, is a fireman whose job is not to put out fires, but to start them by burning books and the houses which contain them. When he becomes aware of the power and importance of books, he begins to read them in secret. Unable to stop their destruction and in grave danger because of what he has done, he joins a group of people who have devised a unique way of preserving the wisdom of the past.

Buck, Pearl. *East Wind: West Wind.* (1930). New York: Thomas Y. Crowell. 277 pp.

Kwei-lan, a young woman from an ancient and honorable Chinese family, tells this story of her marriage to a Chinese man who has adopted Western ways. Her mother has taught her to please her husband and her husband's people according to the customs of the Chinese. But her husband, she finds, has abandoned these customs and considers her his equal; thus they both have difficult adjustments to make. Her brother, who has also adopted the ways of Americans and has brought an American wife back to China with him, also has problems. There are conflicts not only between East and West, but also between age and youth, in this narrative of cross-cultural love.

Burnett, Frances Hodgson. *The Secret Garden.* (1911). London: J. M. Dent. Philadelphia: J. B. Lippincott. 256 pp.

Available in paperback from Heinemann, Penguin, London; Dell, New York.

Mary Lennox, a 9-year-old girl, has moved from India to her uncle's home in England after her mother, her father, and most of their servants have died of cholera. Because Mary has had servants to do everything for her, she has become spoiled and disagreeable. When she moves to England she finds friends; one of them is Dickon, a Yorkshire boy, who understands the wild creatures of the moor. She also discovers Colin, her young cousin, who is ill and thought to be dying. The three children find a garden which is kept locked, and after Mary finds the key, they spend a great deal of time working in it. Eventually they learn why the garden has been locked up. Meanwhile, working in this garden has improved Colin's health and Mary's disposition. Set in Yorkshire, England, this book contains interesting characters, suspense, and a great deal of folk wisdom.
Y

Burnford, Sheila. *The Incredible Journey.* (1961). Boston: Little, Brown, & Co. London: Hodder & Stoughton. 146 pp.

Available in paperback from Paper Jacks, Markham, Ontario; Hodder & Stoughton, London; Bantam, New York.

The characters in this book are three animals: a Siamese cat, an old English bull terrier, and a Labrador retriever. Together, they cross miles of Canadian wilderness in search of their owners. Although they seem to think and sometimes to behave as humans do, their instincts are those of animals. The story, therefore, is believable, even though the journey they take is incredible (unbelievable).
Y

Cather, Willa. *O Pioneers!* (1913). Boston: Houghton Mifflin. 309 pp.

Available in paperback from Houghton Mifflin, Boston; Virago, London.

Set in 19th-century Nebraska, this novel contains characters from numerous European backgrounds: Swedish, Norwegian, Russian, Bohemian. Alexandra Bergson, a competent young woman, takes charge of her family's land after her father's death and looks after the youngest child, Emil. The older boys, Lou and Oscar, though industrious, are less competent than Alexandra.

The story, which covers a period of 20 years, begins when Alexandra is about 20 and Emil is 5. It is filled with dramatic incidents, but the main interest is Alexandra, strong-willed yet tender, independent but sometimes lonely, devoted to her friends and her youngest brother, tolerant of her two narrow-minded older brothers.

Christie, Agatha. *Crooked House.* (1949). London: Collins. New York: Dodd, Mead & Co. 224 pp.

Available in paperback from Fontana, London; Pocket, New York.

Aristide Leonides, who lived in a large home in England with his grown children and grandchildren, has been murdered. He was a widower who had married Brenda, many years younger than he and a prime suspect. Also suspected is Laurence, the tutor of Josephine and

Eustace, Aristide's grandchildren. Other suspects are Aristide's son Roger, and his wife Clemency; Philip, the younger son, and his wife Magda; Aunt Edith de Haviland, the sister of Aristide's first wife; and even Sophia, daughter of Philip and Magda and older sister of Josephine and Eustace. Charles, who narrates the story, is engaged to Sophia, so there is some love interest in this novel, but the main interest is in who committed the murder—actually murders, for as in many mystery novels, more than one person is murdered before the story ends.

Cleaver, Vera, & Cleaver, Bill. *Where the Lilies Bloom.* (1969). New York: Harper & Row. 175 pp.

Available in paperback from New American Library, New York.

When Roy Luther dies, his 14-year-old daughter, Mary Call Luther, takes charge of the family, which consists of an 18-year-old sister whom Mary Call considers "cloudy-headed," an 8-year-old brother, and a 4-year-old sister. Afraid that the county welfare people will separate them, the children tell no one of their father's death. They bury their father on a mountainside, survive by gathering herbs to sell, and with some help from the man who owns the land on which they live, manage to keep their little family together. This is a delightful story of the independence, self-sufficiency, and pride of mountain people and of a brave 14-year-old girl who is not quite as self-sufficient as she thinks she is.
Y

Craven, Margaret. *I Heard the Owl Call My Name.* (1967). New York: Doubleday. London: Heinemann. 166 pp.

Available in paperback from Irwin Publishing, Richmond Hill, Ontario; Totem, Don Mills, Ontario.

Mark Brian, a 27-year-old vicar, is sent by his bishop to the remote village of Kingcome in western British Columbia. In spite of cultural differences he becomes a part of the community, suffering with the Indians at times of birth, death, and the making of difficult decisions. For the younger members of the community, the most serious decision is whether to stay in their ancestral village or move to the larger world of the white man. The book is somewhat sad, but its sadness is relieved by the subtle sense of humor of the members of the Indian tribe.

Emecheta, Buchi. *Second-Class Citizen.* (1974). London: Allison & Busby. New York: Braziller. 175 pp.

Available in paperback from Fontana, London.

Adah, an ambitious Nigerian woman, and her husband Francis move from Lagos to London with disastrous results. Because they are Nigerians, they have trouble finding a home. They also have trouble adjusting to British customs. Adah works to support the family while Francis continues his education, but without much industry or enthusiasm.

In London they are considered second-class citizens because they are black. Both in England and in Nigeria, Adah is considered second-class because she is a woman. The author of this novel is a woman, and the novel is said to be at least in part autobiographical.

Forbes, Kathryn. *Mama's Bank Account.* (1943). New York: Harcourt, Brace. 125 pp.

Available in paperback from HarBrace, Scholastic Book Services, New York.

The narrator is a member of a Norwegian-American family living in San Francisco. The members of the family are Papa, Mama, Nels, Katrin (the narrator), Dagmar, and the baby, Kaaren. There are also numerous aunts and uncles. In each of the 17 short chapters, Mama resolves a crisis or solves a problem. The family's problems are often financial, but because of Mama's careful and clever management and Papa's perseverance, the children all finish high school and college. It is a heart-warming story of immigrants in the first part of this century.

Fritz, Jean. *Brady.* (1960). New York: Coward-McCann. Toronto: Longmans, Breen & Company. 223 pp.

This story takes place before the Civil War in the United States, when many slaves, at great risk, found their way to Canada and freedom by following the North Star. The white people who helped them were also in danger, as helping a slave to escape was a serious crime.

Brady Minton tells his family about some runaway slaves he has seen at a cabin. His father, realizing that by talking about them Brady may be putting the slaves in danger, disapproves of his son's talk. Later, Brady learns about the Underground Railroad, a system of "stations" through which slaves were helped to escape. He begins to understand their situation, and even helps one of them to escape.
Y

George, Jean Craighead. *Julie of the Wolves*. (1972). New York: Harper & Row. Toronto: Fitzhenry & Whiteside. 170 pp.

Available in paperback from Harper & Row, New York; Penguin, London.

Julie's Eskimo name is Miyax. Her mother died when Miyax was very young, and she lives with her father, an Eskimo hunter, until she is 9 years old. Then she is taken by an aunt to be educated, to learn English and how to read. When her father arranges for her to be married at the age of 13, she at first consents, but then runs away and tries to find her way to San Francisco. She gets lost, and makes friends with a wolf pack. This story contains much interesting information about the people and the wild life of Alaska.
Y

Gilman, Dorothy. *A Nun in the Closet*. (1975). Garden City, NY: Doubleday. 191 pp. (op)

Available in paperback from Fawcett, New York.

Two Catholic nuns, Sister John and Sister Hyacinthe, are sent from their convent in Pennsylvania to New York State to see about an estate that their order has received from an unknown donor. When they arrive, they find an enormous old house, completely furnished, and a well full of money, which they believe is a part of the donation to their order. While at the house they meet some young people who seem to be hippies, some migrant workers, and some members of the

"Establishment." To their surprise, they find a wounded man, dressed as a nun, slumped in a closet. The interaction among these oddly assorted characters in this mystery story makes entertaining reading.

Gilman, Dorothy. *Mrs. Pollifax on the China Station.* (1983). Garden City, NY: Doubleday. London: Robert Hale. 192 pp.

Available in paperback from Fawcett, New York.

Emily Pollifax, a middle-aged woman of considerable experience in undertaking dangerous missions for the CIA (Central Intelligence Agency), is sent to China to help a Chinese citizen escape to the West. She travels in China with a tour group, knowing that she has an accomplice in that group but not knowing which of the other tourists he or she is. When the identity of her accomplice is finally revealed, they work together well, and after many exciting adventures they locate the man they are supposed to help. The plot of the novel is the search for this man, but most readers will become equally interested in the behavior of the American tourists and in the descriptions of the Chinese countryside.
M

Godden, Rumer. *The River.* (1946). Boston: Little, Brown & Co. (op) New York: Amereon. London: Chivers. 176 pp.

This story of an English family in Bengal, India, moves as slowly and smoothly as the river beside which the family lives. Harriet, the main character, is a young adolescent. There are three other children and their parents. There are also numerous servants in the household. The family is Christian, at least in name. The servants are of various faiths and classes (Mohammedan, Sikh, Buddhist, Hindu Brahmin, and Hindu untouchable), yet all live harmoniously together. The story contains a death, a birth, guilt, and disappointment, but it also contains moments of joy and happiness. Regardless of what happens, life in the household moves on in quiet order.
M

Godden, Rumer. *The Diddakoi.* (1972). New York: Viking. London: Macmillan. 148 pp.

Available in paperback from Penguin, London.

Kizzy Lovell and her grandmother are gypsies who live in an orchard on the estate of Admiral Twiss. When the grandmother dies, her wagon is burned, according to gypsy custom, and Kizzy runs away, taking her horse Joe with her. After the Admiral takes them in, gossipy and meddlesome neighbors make trouble. Kizzy is also mistreated by the girls in her school, but eventually they learn to appreciate some of her customs, and Kizzy herself adjusts to a different kind of life.
Y

Greene, Graham. *Our Man in Havana*. (1958). London: Heinemann. New York: Viking. 223 pp.

Available in paperback from Heinemann, London; Penguin, New York.

Mr. Wormold, who sells vacuum cleaners in Havana, lives with his 16-year-old daughter Milly, whose mother has left them. When a Mr. Hawthorne appears from London, Wormold unwillingly becomes a secret agent. Although reluctant to become a spy, he adjusts to the situation by lying to Hawthorne and to the people in London whom Hawthorne represents.

The story is a satire on espionage, but Wormold, the reluctant spy, remains a likeable character. Since the people who press him into this deceitful business are themselves deceitful—as is the entire occupation of espionage—Wormold appears innocent by comparison.
M

Harris, Rosemary. *Zed*. (1982). London: Faber & Faber. 185 pp.

Available in paperback from Methuen Children's Books, London.

This beautiful but frightening story, related by Zed when he is about 15 years old, describes his experience at age 8 when he was held as a hostage along with his father, his uncle, and ten other men. His uncle has a son, Ali Baha, a few years younger than Zed, and the children are close friends. One of the terrorists, who has a son about the age of Ali Baha, is kind to Zed during the ordeal. In addition to telling an exciting story, this book contains several important themes: father-son relationships; the behavior of captives and captors under tension; courage and sacrifice; and reconciliation, personal if not political.

Y

Hemingway, Ernest. *The Old Man and the Sea*. (1952). New York: Charles Scribner's Sons. London: Jonathan Cape. London: Heinemann. 140 pp.

Available in paperback from Scribner's, New York; Panther, London.

In this story of courage and defeat, an old fisherman struggles to catch an enormous fish and then to keep it from being consumed by sharks. The author deepens the loneliness of this quest by exploring the old man's relationship with a young fishing companion who is no longer allowed to accompany his aging friend at sea.

Many critics have discussed the symbolism in this novel, but it is possible to read it simply as a tale of one man's noble struggle, of a boy's loyalty and sympathetic concern, and of dignity in defeat.

Hersey, John. *A Bell for Adano*. (1944). New York: Alfred A. Knopf. 269 pp.

Available in paperback from AMSCO School Publications, New New York.

After the Americans occupy the small Italian town of Adano during World War II, Major Victor Joppolo is placed in charge. The author's foreword states that "what [Joppolo] did and what he was not able to do in Adano represented in miniature what America can and cannot do in Europe." The major is almost too wise and too good to be believable, but the other characters, less-than-perfect Italians and Americans, are credible players in a truly entertaining human comedy.

What Major Joppolo did was simply to acquire a new bell for the town. The citizens were grateful.

Hersey, John. *A Single Pebble*. (1956). New York: Alfred A. Knopf. 181 pp.

The narrator, a hydraulics engineer in his early 20s, takes a trip on

the Yangtze River to investigate the possibility of buiding a dam in one of the river's gorges. His traveling companions on the Chinese junk include a strong young man called Old Pebble, who is not only a skillful tracker; he sings while he works and recites poetry with the junk owner's young wife. Like the other trackers, however, he is illiterate and apparently without ambition. Being American, the young engineer cannot understand how the river people can be so contented with their lives. In the course of the long, slow journey, however, he learns much about the Great River Yangtze and the people who work on it. He also learns a great deal about himself and his own values.
M

Ishiguro, Kazuo. *A Pale View of Hills.* (1982). London: Faber and Faber. 183 pp.

Available in paperback from Penguin, New York.

This novel is set in Japan, a few years after the bombing of Nagasaki, and in England, about 26 years later. The narrator is Etsuko, the mother of two daughters; the father of one was Japanese, of the other, English. The older daughter has died before the novel begins. Niki, who is part English and lives with friends in London, visits her mother in her English country home. During Niki's 5-day visit, Etsuko recalls her life in Nagasaki and a neighbor there whose life in many ways paralled her own. The shifts in time and place make the novel sometimes difficult, but reading it is a rewarding experience, as it shows the lasting psychological effects of the war on the Japanese.

The author, a native of Japan, lives in England and writes in English.
M

Jhabvala, Ruth Prawer. *The Householder.* (1963). London: John Murray. 192 pp.

Available in paperback from Penguin, London; W. W. Norton, New York.

Prem, the hero of this story, has all the troubles common to young married men everywhere, and one more: His marriage was arranged by his mother. He is not making enough money to pay his rent, yet he lacks courage to ask for an increase in salary. His wife, with whom he is ill at ease, becomes pregnant. His mother comes to visit, and his wife embarrasses him by leaving to visit her parents. Prem cannot find a friend who will listen to him, for his friends have problems of their own. But he is a "householder," who recognizes his responsibilities as a married man and at times even enjoys them.

Kemelman, Harry. *Friday the Rabbi Slept Late*. (1964). New York: G. P. Putnam's Sons. 160 pp.

Available in paperback from Fawcett, Greenwich, CT.

Who is the murderer of Elspeth Bleech, the young girl who lived at the home of the Serapinos and took care of their children? Is it the children's father? Is it Melvin Bronstein, whose car was seen parked in front of the Serapino house late on the evening of the murder? Is it Stanley Doble, the janitor at the Jewish temple? Is it Rabbi David Small, in whose car Elspeth's purse was found? The rabbi not only establishes his own innocence and that of at least one other suspect, but by using the ability to reason which he has acquired from his scholarly study of the Talmud, reveals to the police who the real murderer is.

Other books in which this clever young rabbi solves a mystery are: *Saturday the Rabbi Went Hungry*, *Sunday the Rabbi Stayed Home*, *Monday the Rabbi Took Off*, *Tuesday the Rabbi Saw Red*, *Wednesday the Rabbi Got Wet*, and *Thursday the Rabbi Walked Out*.

Knowles, John. *A Separate Peace*. (1959). New York: Macmillan. London: Heinemann. Richmond Hill, Ontario: Irwin. 186 pp.

Available in paperback from Bantam, New York, Toronto, London, Sydney, Auckland; Dell, New York.

Set in a boys preparatory school in New Hampshire during World War II, this thought-provoking novel deals with friendship and tragedy. The main characters are Eugene Forrester, a good student, and his roommate Phineas ("Finny"), an excellent athlete who frequently leads Eugene and the other boys in games and adventures, usually dangerous and always against the school rules. While Finny is directing one of these pranks, his leg is broken, and Eugene blames himself, not without reason. The accident itself is less important than the ways in which the boys react to it.

L'Engle, Madeleine. *Meet the Austins*. (1960). New York: Vanguard. (op) 192 pp.

Available in paperback from Dell, New York.

The Austin family consists of a father, a mother, and four children, who are 5, 10, 12, and 15 years old. Vicky, who narrates the story, is 12. When Maggie, who is 11, comes to stay with the family, the household is upset. Maggie's father has been killed in a plane wreck, and her mother has been dead for several years, so she is an orphan and an only child, unaccustomed to living in a large family. The plot reveals how she adjusts to the Austin family and how they adjust to her. Some of the episodes in the book are amusing, some are exciting, and all reveal the warmth and concern for one another found in a happy family.
Y

Lessing, Doris. *The Grass is Singing*. (1950). New York: Thomas Y. Crowell Co. (op) 245 pp.

Available in paperback from New American Library, New York.

Dick Turner, an unsuccessful farmer in South Africa, has many problems. One of the most serious is his wife Mary's treatment of the natives who work for them. This novel carefully considers Mary's reactions to her husband, to the farm, to the neighbors, and to the natives. It is the story of one woman's inability to adjust to another culture and a chilling commentary on race relations in South Africa.
M

Lewis, C. S. *Out of the Silent Planet*. (1943). New York: MacMillan. 174 pp.

Available in paperback from Pan, London; Macmillan, New York.

Two Englishmen kidnap a third and transport him to the planet of Malacandra, where he meets and befriends *seroni* (or sorns), *brossa*, and *pfftriggi*, the three distinct intelligent species that inhabit the planet. This is utopian science fiction, based on Christian principles.
M

Lewis, C. S. *The Lion, the Witch, and the Wardrobe*. (1950). London: Collins. New York: Macmillan. 154 pp.

Available in paperback from Armada, London; Dell, New York.

By entering a wardrobe, four children find their way to the land of Narnia. This country is held under a constant winter and ruled by the cruel White Witch, who symbolizes evil. A great lion called Aslan symbolizes good. Other characters include talking beasts who befriend the children as well as creatures who are loyal to the White Witch. The book contains vivid descriptions of bloody battles between the good and evil forces, with good conquering in the end.
This book is part of a series called *The Chronicles of Narnia*. Others in the series are *Prince Caspian, The Voyage of the Dawn Treader, The Silver Chair, The Horse and His Boy, The Magician's Nephew,* and *The Last Battle*.
Y

Markandaya, Kamala. *Nectar in a Seive*. (1954). New York: John Day. (op)

Available in paperback from New Amerian Library, New York; Lakshmi, New Delhi. 189 pp.

The setting is India. Rukmani is married to a tenant farmer, Nathan, who is "poor in everything but in love and care" for her. He is devoted to the land, but he cannot persuade any of his four sons to work with him at farming. This is a moving story of poverty and love.

Markandaya, Kamala. *A Handful of Rice*. (1966). London: Hamish Hamilton. New York: Thomas Y. Crowell. 237 pp.

Available in paperback from Orient Paperbacks and Hind Pocket Books, New Delhi.

Ravi leaves his home in a village in India to try to escape poverty and to seek his fortune in a city. First he meets Damadar, who teaches him how to earn a dishonest living. Then he meets Apu, from whom he learns the tailor's trade. When he becomes a member of Apu's household he is happy with his life but discontented with the

crowded living arrangements. After Apu's death, Ravi struggles to keep the business going and support the family, but economic conditions, the arrogance of his customers, the customs of bribery and bargaining, and the indolence of other members of the household make escape from poverty impossible.
M

Michener, James A. *The Bridges at Toko-Ri*. (1953). New York: Random House.

Available in paperback from Fawcett, New York; Corgi Books, Socker & Warburt, London.

The hero of this tale of brave men is Harry Brubaker, a reluctant American participant in the Korean War who nevertheless does his duty bravely and efficiently, as do his comrades. A navy fighter pilot, he depends on his fellow fighter pilots, helicopter pilots, and the crew members of carriers. The emphasis is on the interdependence of these men and their loyalty to each other in a war which is practically ignored by their country.
M

Moberg, Vilhelm. *Unto a Good Land*. (1953). (Gustaf Lannestock, Trans.). New York: Simon & Schuster. (op). (Original work published 1952). 309 pp.

Available in paperback from Warner, New York.

Karl Oskar Nilsson, his wife Kristina, their three small children, and Karl Oskar's brother Robert are among a group of fifteen Swedish immigrants who land in New York in the spring of 1850. All members of the group travel by steamboat, train, and foot to the territory of Minnesota. Not only is the trip extremely difficult; settling in the new land requires unbelievably hard work, and the Nilsson family suffers from the cold and the scarcity of food. This story of early settlers in North America is filled with suspense, excitement, and gentle humor.

This novel is the second book of a trilogy. The first is *The Emigrants*, which is set in Sweden and describes the conditions there which caused the family to emigrate. The third is *Last Letter Home*, which tells more of the life of the family in the New World.

Narayan, R. K. *The English Teacher*. (1945). London: Eyre & Spottiswoode. (op) London: Heinemann. 184 pp.

Available in paperback from University of Chicago, Chicago.

The narrator is Krishna, a 30-year-old lecturer in English at Albert Mission College. When his wife Susila and infant daughter Leena join him, their life is happy. Susila is a good wife and manager, the child is healthy and happy, and Krishna is devoted to them both. But tragedy strikes, and his life changes. He makes two close friends: a farmer, who introduces him to a band of spirits and a psychic experience; and the headmaster of a children's school, who influences him to follow a more satisfying, though less remunerative, way of life. This moving novel is sometimes sad, sometimes humorous. It holds the reader's interest, though one may be puzzled at times by the beliefs and behavior of the characters.

Narayan, R. K. *A Tiger for Malgudi*. (1982). New York: Viking. 175 pp.

Available in paperback from Penguin, New York and London.

Raja, a magnificent tiger, is the central character and narrator of this unusual novel. He frequently examines his own behavior as well as that of the other animals and the humans by whom he is surrounded. Most important of the human characters are Captain, an animal trainer who understands Raja far better than do most humans but whose understanding is nevertheless limited, and a mysterious man called simply "the Master," who exhibits a much deeper understanding of the tiger and subdues him without using violence.

The plot is exciting, the characters are believable, and the philosophy expressed in the book is fascinating.

O'Dell, Scott. *The Black Pearl*. (1967). Boston: Houghton Mifflin. 140 pp.

Available in paperback from Dell, New York.

The narrator, Ramón Salazar, is 16 years old and the son of Blas Salazar, a pearl dealer in Mexico. When Ramón becomes a pearl

diver for his father, he wants to find the Pearl of Heaven in order to impress Gaspar Ruiz, who constantly brags about what he has done. Ramón does find the pearl, but the result is tragedy, believed to be caused by the manta Diablo, a beast who brings misfortune to anyone who displeases him. What really causes the tragedy, however, is the overconfidence of Blas Salazar. Through his father's mistake, young Ramón learns the difference between a bribe and a gift of love.
Y

O'Dell, Scott. *The Captive.* (1979). Boston: Houghton Mifflin. 211 pp.

Julián Escobar, a young man studying to be a priest, reluctantly accompanies Don Luis Arroyo, a wealthy Spanish gentleman, on a trip to the New World. Don Luis travels in search of gold; Julián is supposed to save the souls of the Indians. Because of the greed and poor judgement of Don Luis, the ship is wrecked and the crew members are drowned, but Julián survives and reaches the shore. A young girl finds Julián and teaches him the Mayan language. Then he meets Cantú, a Spanish dwarf, who persuades him to pretend to be the Mayan god Kukulcán.

Readers who enjoy this historical novel may wish to read its sequels: *The Feathered Serpent,* which describes the coming of Cortes to Mexico, and *The Amethyst Ring,* about the fall of the Mayan and Incan civilizations. All three novels are set in Mexico.
Y

Paton, Alan. *Cry, the Beloved Country: A Story of Comfort in Desolation.* (1948). New York: Charles Scribner's Sons. 273 pp.

Available in paperback from Penguin, London.

Stephen Kumalo, an elderly black pastor in a small South African village, travels to Johannesburg in search of his sons and his sister. His personal tragedy unfolds against a background of broken tribal and family ties and forgotten moral values. Yet, as its subtitle indicates, the novel is "a story of comfort in desolation," for Kumalo finds strength in his religious faith and through the compassion of others, including a white farmer from whom sympathy might be least expected.
M

Rachlin, Nahid. *Foreigner.* (1978). New York: W. W. Norton & Company. 192 pp.

Available in paperback from W. W. Norton, New York.

Feri, an Iranian woman who has lived in the United States for 14 years and who is married to an American, goes to visit her family in Iran. While there she realizes how strong the ties are which bind her to her native country and her people. She is forced to choose between returning to Boston, her job, her husband, and the rapid, time-conscious way of life to which she thought she had become accustomed and remaining in an Iranian village, where life is slower and more relaxed.

Rachlin, Nahid. *Married to a Stranger.* (1983). New York: E. P. Dutton, Inc. 220 pp.

Available from Clarke, Irwing & Co., Toronto and Vancouver.

This novel is set in Iran, from the mid-1970s until after the overthrow of the Shah. Minou Hakimi marries her high school teacher, Javad Partovi, with whom she is very much in love, but finds the marriage bitterly disappointing. Javad is kind to her, but she feels neglected. Slowly she becomes aware that he is unfaithful to her.
The reader gets interesting insights into life in Iran during the reign of the Shah: the resentment of the very religious Moslems against the influence of the West; the position of women; the contrast between the attitudes of younger and older generations.
M

Remarque, Erich Maria. *All Quiet on the Western Front.* (1929). (A. W. Wheen, Trans.). New York: Little, Brown & Co. London: Heinemann. (original work published 1928). 236 pp.

Available in paperback from Mayflower, London; Fawcett, New York.

Paul Baumer and three of his classmates, all 19 years old, have volunteered for the German Army in World War I. The experiences of these four young men and their friends are the subject of of this novel: the horrors of gas, hand-to-hand fighting in the trenches, hunger, constant bombardment, the screams of the wounded and the inadequate facilities for treating them. Written over 50 years ago, this book remains the classic anti-war novel of the century.

Richter, Conrad. *The Light in the Forest*. (1953). New York: Alfred A. Knopf. 117 pp.

Available in paperback from Bantam, Toronto; New York; London; and Sydney.

Johnny Butler is captured by Indians when he is 4 years old and raised as one of them; he is called True Son. When he is 15, he is sent back to his white parents, but he cannot adjust to the ways of the white people. He escapes with the help of his cousin, Half Arrow, and returns to Indian land, where he is faced with the dilemma of betraying either the Whites or the Indians.

This novel introduces the reader to the values of native Americans. It also shows the problems confronted when one must choose between two cultures.
Y

Saint Exupéry, Antoine de. *Night Flight*. (1932). (S. Gilbert, Trans.). (original work published 1931). 87 pp.

Available in paperback from Harcourt Brace, New York and London; Penguin, London.

This is a story of brave men involved in the dangerous work of flying the mail at night during the early days of air mail service. They are Fabian, a pilot bringing mail from Patagonia to Buenos Aires; Rivière, who is in charge of operations; Pellerin, another pilot; and Robineau, the inspector. It is a touching account of courage in daily life.
M

Saint Exupéry, Antoine de. *The Little Prince*. (1943). (K. Woods, Trans.). New York: Harcourt Brace. London: Heinemann. (original work published 1943). 111 pp.

Available in paperback from Piccolo, Pan, London; HarBrace, New York.

The narrator, a pilot, has an airplane accident in the desert. A little prince appears and relates the details of life on his tiny planet, his visits to other asteroids, and his adventures on the planet Earth. On each asteroid he finds one person living alone and keeping busy doing something which he considers of consequence. On the planet Earth, which he visits last, the prince meets numerous men of these occupations, all busy working but somehow missing what is really important.

This whimsical fable can be read at different levels: by children as a simple story, and by mature readers for its thought-provoking ideas.

(op) Sarton, May. *Joanna and Ulysses.* (1963). New York: W. W. Norton. 127 pp.

Joanna, a 30-year-old Athenian woman, takes a vacation on the Greek island of Santorini, where she buys a weak and wounded donkey because she feels sorry for him. She names him Ulysses and nurses him back to health, then must decide what to do with him when she returns home to Athens. The story is a delightful mixture of sadness and humor.

Schaefer, Jack. *Shane.* (1949). Boston: Houghton Mifflin. (op) 119 pp.

Available in paperback from Bantam, New York; Toronto; London; and Sydney. Illustrated juvenile edition available from Houghton Mifflin, Boston. 214 pp.

This novel belongs to a uniquely American *genre,* the "western." The plot is based on the conflict between the homesteaders, who fence in their property and farm it, and the cattlemen, who want their cattle to be able to graze freely over the land.

The hero, Shane, rides on his horse to the homestead of Joe Starrett, his wife, and his young son Bob. Starrett and Shane become good friends, and young Bob admires Shane as much as he admires his father. Shane helps Starrett in his conflict with Fletcher, the leader of the cattlemen. The book contains numerous physical conflicts, including an account of a fist fight in which Shane is greatly outnumbered and a gunfight in which he is wounded.

Shute, Nevil. *A Town Like Alice*. (1950). London: William Heinemann. New York: William Morrow. (op) New York and Toronto: Random House. 277 pp.

Available in paperback from Pan, London; Random House of Canada, Toronto; Ballantine, New York.

Set primarily in Malaysia and Australia, this novel begins in the early years of World War II and covers a period of approximately 10 years. Jean Paget, a courageous and resourceful young English woman who speaks the Malay language fluently, is indispensable to a group of British women who are being marched by the Japanese from place to place. The Japanese are kind to the children and never brutal to their charges; in fact, the guards and the prisoners take care of each other, until the last guard dies and the women take refuge in a Malayan village. Later, when Jean marries Joe Harman, an Australian, and lives in his country, her resourcefulness is again evident.

This gripping novel is based in part on an event which actually occured, not in Malaysia but in Indonesia.

Steinbeck, John. *The Pearl*. (1945). New York: Viking. London: Heinemann. 118 pp.

Available in paperback from Bantam, New York; London; Sydney; and Toronto; Pan, London.

Kino, a poor fisherman, finds a valuable pearl which he hopes to be able to sell and thus be able to make a better life for himself, his wife Juana, and their little son Coyotito. However, the pearl brings only tragedy to this unfortunate family in Mexico.

Steinbeck, John. *The Short Reign of Pippin IV: A Fabrication*. (1967). New York: Viking. (op) London: Heinemann. 188 pp.

Available in paperback from Penguin, New York; Pan, London.

France has decided that the French Revolution was a mistake and that the monarchy should be restored. But who will be the monarch? When the throne is offered to Pippin, an amateur astronomer, he reluctantly accepts. The story describes Pippin's actions as king, his wife's problems with housekeeping in a palace, and their daughter Clotilde's romance with Ted Johnson, whose father, "the Egg King of Petaluma," owns a successful poultry business in Petaluma, California. This is an amusing, slightly satirical story.

Stewart, Mary. *The Moon-Spinners*. (1962). London: Hodder & Stoughton. New York: M. S. Mill & Morrow. (op) 303 pp.

Available in paperback from Hodder, London; Fawcett, New York.

Set on the island of Crete, this exciting adventure tale includes murder, intrigue, smuggling, and frightening encounters on land and sea. Nicola Ferris, a young Englishwoman, is to meet her cousin Frances at a village where they are to spend a week vacationing. When Frances arrives, Nicola has become involved in the problems of Mark Langley, who has been wounded by gunshot and whose 15-year-old brother, Colin, has been kidnapped. The search for Colin, the attempts to find out who is responsible for wounding Mark, and the budding romance between Mark and Nicola keep the reader eager to know what will happen next. Interlaced with the excitement are excellent descriptions of the countryside, especially of the wildflowers.

Tyler, Anne. *Dinner at the Homesick Restaurant*. (1982). New York: Alfred A. Knopf. Toronto: Random House of Canada. London: Chatto & Windus. 303 pp.

Available in paperback from Alfred A. Knopf, New York; Berkley, New York; Penguin, London; Random House, Toronto.

This novel is about the problems of a 20th-century American family. Pearl, the mother, is efficient, domineering, and often cruel. Beck, the father, leaves home when the three children are young. Cody, the oldest child, is jealous of his younger brother Ezra and torments him both as a child and as an adult, but Ezra is patient, kind, and forgiving. Jenny, the youngest, eventually learns to deal with her problems, not always wisely, by laughing at them. The book is sometimes sad, sometimes funny, sometimes both at once.
M

Uchida, Yoshiko. *Journey Home.* (1978). New York: Atheneum. Toronto: McClelland & Stewart. 131 pp.

Available in paperback from Atheneum, New York.

Twelve-year-old Yuki and her parents have moved back to Berkeley, California, after being kept in a relocation center for people of Japanese ancestry during World War II. Living in the camp was difficult; returning to their former life is not easy, either. Yuki's father cannot find a job, many people hate the Japanese, and it is hard for the family to find a place to live. Yuki's brother Ken, who has fought with a United States regiment in Italy, returns home wounded and embittered. Gradually, however, things get better for this family.
The author was born in California and lived in a relocation center during the war. She writes of this unfortunate chapter in American history with sensitivity and without bitterness.
This book is a sequel to *Journey to Topaz,* which is about the family's internment in the relocation center.
Y

Voight, Cynthia. *Homecoming.* (1981). New York: Atheneum. 320 pp.

Available in paperback from Fawcett, Ballantine, New York; Random House of Canada, Toronto.

The mother of the four Timmerman children leaves them in the car parked in a shopping center in a small Connecticut town. After waiting many hours for her to return, the children decide to walk to their great aunt's house in Bridgeport. Dicey, the oldest at 13, takes charge. They sleep in parks, in cemeteries, in deserted buildings, and often camp beside water so they can fish. Occasionally Dicey gets a job and they can buy groceries. Her one desire is to keep the family together and out of foster homes. It is not an easy task, and they are often hungry. When they reach their destination, they encounter further problems.
A sequel, *Dicey's Song,* tells of the life of the four children after they reach their grandmother's farm in Maryland.
Y

Wartski, Maureen Crane. *A Boat to Nowhere.* (1980). Philadelphia: Westminster. 191 pp.

Available in paperback from New American Library, New York.

Kien, a young Vietnamese boy, has always lived by his wits and does not make friends easily. When he arrives in a coastal village, he does not adjust well; but he proves himself useful, and the villagers learn to trust him. They allow him to take the only boat, the *Sea Breeze*, to bring in fish for the community. Later, Kien, two other children, and a grandfather escape in the *Sea Breeze* from government representatives who have threatened to take the grandfather away. They suffer many hardships and have some narrow escapes. Throughout their adventures, the wisdom of the grandfather, the quick wit of Kien, and the courage of the two children are apparent.
Y

Wartski, Maureen Crane. *A Long Way From Home*. (1980). Philadelphia: Westminster. 155 pp.

Available in paperback from New American Library, New York.

Kien, a 15-year-old Vietnamese refugee, goes to live with Steve and Diane Olson in Bradley, California. He has trouble adjusting to the Olsons' household and resents having to go to school. He runs away to Travor, a fishing town, and stays with Vietnamese people there. Unfortunately, there is trouble between the American fishermen and the newly-arrived immigrants from Southeast Asia. How Kien gets involved in this dispute and helps to reconcile the two groups of fishermen makes exciting reading.
Y

Waters, Frank. *The Man Who Killed the Deer*. (1941). New York: Farrar & Rinehart. (op) Chicago and London: Swallow. Athens, OH: Ohio University. (op) 266 pp.

Available in paperback from Washington Square, New York; Pocket, New York.

Martiniano has been sent to the "away school" provided by the U.S. government for Indians living on reservations. When he returns to his tribe several years later, the elders of his people are not pleased with the way in which his education has changed him. He will not participate in the dances; he has learned to irrigate a field instead of dancing for rain. He also defies the laws of the white man by killing a deer out of season. This novel will deepen the reader's understanding of native Americans and their unique way of looking at the world.

White, E. B. *Charlotte's Web.* (1952). New York and London: Harper & Row. (Hardcover and paperback). 184 pp.

Fern Arable persuades her father, a farmer, not to kill a little pig but to let her raise it as a pet. But after a few months, Wilbur, the pig, is in danger of losing his life and being turned into ham and bacon. Charlotte, a clever spider who lives in the barn with Wilbur and several other farm animals not only saves Wilbur's life but also makes him an outstanding attraction at the county fair. The animals talk to each other in an amusing way, and Fern is the only human who can understand them.
This charming tale contains much wit and wisdom which adults will enjoy as well as children.
Y

Wibberley, Leonard. *The Mouse That Roared.* (1954). Boston: Little, Brown & Co. 280 pp.

Available in paperback from Bantam, New York.

The tiny duchy of Grand Fenwick faces a financial crisis. Its main source of income is the production of wine, and it discovers that a cheap imitation of its wine is being produced in California. The duchy uses this situation as a reason for declaring war on the United States, although it actually wishes to be defeated and afterwards rehabilitated by the United States.
The U.S. State Department, which at first ignores the declaration of war, becomes alarmed when the yeomen from Grand Fenwick kidnap the inventor of the Q-bomb and take him and the bomb back to Grand Fenwick. The tiny duchy has suddenly become a world power, acquiring all of the problems that beset a powerful nation. This is excellent satire.

Wilder, Thornton. *The Bridge of San Luis Rey.* (1927). New York: Grosset & Dunlap. (op) 235 pp.

Reprint edition available from Harper & Row. Available in paperback from Avon, New York; Washington Square, New York.

Five people were killed when a bridge in Peru collapsed on July 20, 1714. In this novel Brother Juniper investigates their lives and attempts to discover why these particular people died at that particular time. This is a thought-provoking book.
M

Yep, Laurence. *Dragonwings*. (1975). New York: Harper & Row. 256 pp.

Available in paperback from Harper & Row, New York; Fitzhenry & Whiteside, Toronto.

This book tells of a young boy who leaves China to join his father, who works in a laundry in San Francisco and dreams of flying like a dragon. It is based on a historical incident: In 1909 a young Chinese flier kept his biplane in the air for 20 minutes over Oakland, California. Other events in the story are for the most part fictitious, but the conditions surrounding them—for example, the San Francisco earthquake of 1906—are real.

The relations of the Chinese immigrants to each other and to the white "demons", both good and bad, and the differences between the customs of the two groups of people, are depicted carefully and accurately.
Y

Yep, Laurence. *The Serpent's Children*. (1984). New York: Harper & Row. Toronto: Fitzhenry & Whiteside. 277 pp.

The setting is 19th-century China. Cassia, the narrator, is 8 years old when her mother dies, telling the child to take care of her father and her younger brother Foxfire. The family is threatened by famine and bandits: The country is struggling against Manchu and British domination. As the children grow older, Foxfire and the father have serious disagreements about what is important in life and how they should try to solve their problems. This emotion-packed novel will hold the reader's interest to the end.
Y

Nonfiction

Adamson, Joy. *Born Free: A Lioness of Two Worlds.* (1960). New York: Pantheon. London: Collins. 220 pp.

Available in paperback from Fontana, London; Random House, New York.

The author and her husband, a game warden in Kenya, adopted a lion cub whose mother had been killed and named her Elsa. The Adamsons gave Elsa excellent care, and she adjusted well to her life with humans. Nevertheless, there came a time when she had to be returned to her natural home. The Adamsons released her gradually and made sure that she would be able to survive without their care. Elsa was reluctant to leave them but finally understood that she must. At the time the book was written there was no other record of a lion which had been tamed and then successfully returned to the jungle.

Alireza, Marianne. *At the Drop of a Veil.* (1971). Boston: Houghton Mifflin. 275 pp.

The author, a native Californian, married an Arabian student and went to live with him and his large family in his country. Her adjustment to the customs of her adopted land were not easy. She had to wear a veil; she was not permitted to move freely outside the house; she had to learn the language; and she had to become accustomed to a culture very different from her own. Fortunately, her husband's many relatives were considerate and understanding, and she writes of them all with affection. Nevertheless, there were some embarrassing and amusing incidents, which she relates in a lively and entertaining manner.

Anonymous. *Go Ask Alice.* (1971). Englewood Cliffs, NJ: Prentice-Hall. 188 pp.

Available in paperback from Avon, New York.

This book is based on the diary of a 15-year-old girl who became addicted to drugs. It begins with accounts of her school, her friends, and her family's move to another city, where she felt lonely and insecure. When she met other young people who took drugs she became addicted, without realizing at first what was happening to her. Inevitably, she became a "pusher"; she sold drugs to others in order to support her own habit. Unfortunately, her story is not unusual, but the account written by this girl shows the reader more effectively than any number of news accounts the temptations that today's young people face.

Asimov, Isaac. *How Did We Find Out About Outer Space?* (1977). New York: Walker and Company. Toronto: Fitzhenry & Whiteside. 59 pp.

Available in paperback from Avon, New York.

This book combines clear explanations of scientific principles with occasional references to related mythology and literature. It contains five chapters: Flying, Vacuum, Rockets, Liquid-Fuel Rockets, and Satellites and Spaceships. It can be a useful learning tool for students whose knowledge of English is slight but who are familiar with the scientific principles described, for students who have achieved fluency in English but whose knowledge of science is limited, or for students limited both in the knowledge of science and the knowledge of English. Though written for young people, it is also interesting to mature readers.
Y

Baker, Russell. *Growing Up.* (1982). New York: Congdon & Weed. London: Sidgwick & Jackson. 278 pp.

Available in paperback from the New American Library, New York.

This memoir, which covers the first half of the 20th century, shows the effects of the Great Depression and of World War II on the author's family. It contains vivid and amusing descriptions of his relatives, and especially of his mother, who is determined that her son will "make something of himself." He recognizes the fact that his mother dominates him, but does not resent it.
Written by a popular humorist whose writing appears in leading magazines and newspapers, this book will give readers insight into American values and family life.

Bernstein, Jeremy. *Einstein*. (1973). New York: Viking. (op) 242 pp.

Available in paperback from Penguin, New York; Fontana, London.

This study of Einstein's work and personality will be of interest not only to physics majors, but also to readers with a limited science background. Though he was born in Germany, this quiet, modest man spent much of his life in Switzerland. In 1933, at the age of 54, he moved to the United States to teach at Princeton University, where he stayed for 22 years.

Bernstein explains the quantum theory, the theory of relativity, and the relationship of this last discovery to experiments of other scientists, for whom Einstein always showed a great respect, even when he disagreed with them.

A short bibliography lists Einstein's principal writings and selected books about him.

Boeri, David. *People of the Ice Whale: Eskimos, White Men, & the Whale*. (1983). New York: E. P. Dutton. 280 pp.

Available in paperback from Harcourt Brace, New York.

For three consecutive years the author spent a week or more in the village of Gambell, located on St. Lawrence Island in the Bering Strait. He also spent some time in Barrow, Alaska, described as "the top of the world." He learned to know the Eskimos well, and he writes of them and the whales, which their people have hunted for "as long as their legends recall," with sensitivity and scrupulous honesty. Included in the book are insights into the problems of the clashing of old and new cultures as the Eskimos are introduced to modern ways, conflicting views by state and federal governments and by the International Whaling Commission concerning subsistence whaling in Alaska, and the attempts to resolve these conflicts.

Carter, Jimmy. *The Blood of Abraham: Insights into the Middle East*. (1985). Boston: Houghton Mifflin. 208 pp.

Available in paperback from Houghton Mifflin, Boston.

The author visited the Middle East before, during, and after his

term as President of the United States (1976-1980). In this account he examines the history of the area, going back to Biblical times; the attitudes of the peoples and of their leaders; the relations of these countries with the United States and with the Soviet Union; the possibilities for peace in the future. Israel, Syria, Lebanon, Jordan, Egypt, Saudi Arabia, and the Palestinians are discussed. Interspersed with accounts of the political situations are occasional amusing anecdotes of Mr. Carter's adventures as a distinguished tourist.
M

Cavanagh, Frances. *Jenny Lind and Her Listening Cat.* (1961). New York: Vanguard. 158 pp.

The subject of this biography is a world-famous singer who lived early in the 20th century. She was a lonely child until she went to live with the Anderssons. There she was happier, as she was near her grandmother and she also had the company of a kitten. She often sang to the kitten, and when people heard her they stopped to listen. When the maid of a dancer at the opera house heard Jenny, she took the child to meet her mistress, who arranged for her to take singing lessons. That was the beginning of a successful career. This is a moving account of a child with a special talent.
Y

Clarke, Arthur C. *The Exploration of Space.* (1951). London: Temple. (op) New York: Harper & Row. (op) (1979).

Revised edition available in paperback from Pocket, New York. 233 pp.

In a preface to the 1979 edition the author explains that because of the accuracy of this book's forecasts, he has not updated it. "Only in the chapters on the Moon and planets has this book become seriously dated," he states, "—and that, of course, is as a result of the developments it foretold."
The book begins with a summary of early romantic accounts of imaginary flights in space, then discusses our solar system and the possibilities of travel to other planets in it. Matters such as the construction of rockets and space ships are also discussed. The last chapters discuss the possibilities of travel outside our solar system.
M

Collins, Michael. *Flying to the Moon and Other Strange Places.* (1976). New York: Farrar, Straus and Giroux. 159 pp.

Available in paperback from Farrar, Straus and Giroux, New York.

The author tells of his early days as an Air Force test pilot and of his life as an astronaut. He describes in detail the flight of Apollo 11 to the moon, during which he piloted the command module *Columbia* while Neil Armstrong and Buzz Aldrin were landing on the moon in the lunar module *Eagle*. He describes life on space ships; the earth, the moon, and the stars as seen from outer space; and the excitement of being a part of the space program. Finally, he makes some fascinating predictions for the future of space travel.
Y

Deford, Frank. *Alex: The Life of a Child.* (1983). New York: Viking. 205 pp.

Available in paperback from New American Library, New York.

Born with cystic fibrosis, Alex lived only 8 years. Yet she was a happy child, whose courage was admired by adults and by other children who knew her. The author is her father, and their close relationship is an important part of the book, as are Alex's relationships to her mother and her older brother Chris.

There is still no cure for cystic fibrosis, a genetic disease which kills its victims early in life, but the courageous way in which the Deford family confronted their tragedy will have an impact on anyone who reads this book.

Frank, Anne. *Anne Frank: The Diary of a Young Girl.* (1952). (B. M. Mooyart, Translator). Garden City, NY: Doubleday. (original work published 1952). 308 pp.

Available in paperback from Washington Square, New York; Eiko-Sha, Tokyo. (English edition with Japanese annotations).

Anne's diary begins in June 1942, when she was 13 years old, and ends in August 1944, when she was 15. It describes the life of her parents, her sister, herself, and four others who hide in an office building to escape deportation from occupied Holland, because they were Jews, during World War II. Although life in the "Secret Annex" is tedious, and occasionally the diary itself becomes a little dull, the reader becomes involved in the suspense, the suffering, and the difficult personal adustments of the people living together, forced to maintain silence, often getting on each other's nerves, never able to relax their vigilance.

Fritz, Jean. *Homesick: My Own Story.* (1982). New York: G. P. Putnam's Sons. 163 pp.

Available in paperback from Dell, New York.

This story of the author's life in China as a young girl is basically true, though the author admits that she added some fictional bits when her memory failed her. Born in China of American parents, she learned to speak Chinese at the same time that she learned English. Although the family had some good Chinese friends, there was much hatred in China for "foreign devils." When the family moved back to Pennsylvania, where her grandparents lived, Jean was confronted with the other side of prejudice: Her playmates made unkind remarks about the Chinese. The loyalty and affection that she felt for both countries is apparent throughout the book.
Y

Fritz, Jean. *China Homecoming.* (1985). New York: G. P. Putnam's Sons. 140 pp.

When the author was in her 60s she went back to Wuhan, China, where she had been born and lived until she was 13 years old, and which she considered her "home town." She relates her reactions to the country of her birth, telling of her visits to places she knew as a child: the house in which she lived, the church she attended (now a school for acrobats), the cemetery where her sister was buried (now a children's playground). A great deal of Chinese history, both ancient and modern, is included. Her deep love for China is obvious.

Gilbreth, Frank B., Jr. & Carey, Ernestine G. *Cheaper by the Dozen.* (1948). New York: Harper & Row. (op) 237 pp. New York: Amereon.

Reprint edition available from Amereon, Bantam, and Pocket, New York; Heinemann, London.

This amusing account is about the 14 members of the Gilbreth family: the father, an industrial engineer specializing in time and motion studies; the mother, also an industrial engineer; and their 12 children. Mr. Gilbreth applied his ideas on saving time to the raising of children, who were required to skip grades in school and to learn foreign languages by listening to tapes while taking their baths.

When they became teenagers they rebelled against their father's strict discipline, but their problems were always resolved with good humor. A sequel, *Belles on Their Toes,* describes life in the Gilbreth family after the death of the father in 1924.

(op) Gruber, Ruth. *Felisa Rincón de Gautier: The Mayor of San Juan.* (1972). New York: Thomas Y. Crowell. New York: Dell. 175 pp.

This biography covers the life of Doña Felisa from her childhood until her retirement from political life after serving as mayor of San Juan, Puerto Rico for 22 years. We see her grow from an obedient, unselfish child to a woman concerned about the welfare of all people and especially for the poor. The story of her life includes also the history of Puerto Rico from the time it became a possession of the United States until it received Commonwealth status in 1952.
Y

Hareven, Tamara K. *Eleanor Roosevelt: An American Conscience.* (1968). Chicago: Quadrangle. (op) 311 pp.

Reprint edition available from Da Capo, New York.

Written by a foreign student in American history, this biography emphasizes Mrs. Roosevelt's work, her ideas, and her political and social activities. During the Depression, she was concerned with poverty among coal miners and other workers. She supported legislation that would defend the rights of Blacks in the United States.

During World War II she traveled and visited hospitalized soldiers. Through magazine and newspaper articles she expressed her views on social and economic subjects at home and abroad. After the war she worked for human rights and was active in the United Nations. She

was especially concerned with the issue of human rights and with the dignity of man.
M

Hautzig, Esther. *The Endless Steppe: Growing Up in Siberia.* (1968). New York: Harper & Row. Toronto: Fitzhenry & Whiteside. (op) 243 pp.

Available in paperback from School Book Service, Scholastic. (subtitle *A Girl in Exile*), Penguin, G. K. Hall, New York; Heinemann Educational, Hamilton, London.

During World War II, the author, then 10 years old, and several members of her family were deported from their home in the village of Vilna, Poland. Esther, her parents, and her grandparents were sent to Siberia. The father was later sent away and the grandfather died, but Esther, her mother, and her grandmother stayed there for 5 years, until the end of the war. This is a story of hardships, courage, good humor, and the ability to survive.
Y

Hersey, John. *Hiroshima.* (1946). New York: Alfred A. Knopf. 117 pp.

Available in paperback from Bantam, New York; Penguin, London.

After the atomic bomb was dropped on Hiroshima, the *New Yorker* magazine assigned John Hersey to write a report about it. He went to Hiroshima, where he talked with six survivors: a young woman clerk, a German Jesuit priest, two doctors, a tailor's widow, and a Methodist minister. The result of Hersey's conversations was a detailed account of what happened on August 6, 1945, and in the months following. He writes objectively, simply describing what happened; no additional comments are needed when devastation is so great.

Huxley, Elspeth. *The Flame Trees of Thika: Memories of an African Childhood.* (1959). 288 pp.

Available in paperback from Penguin, London; New York; Ringwood, Victoria, Australia; Markham, Ontario; Auckland, New Zealand.

Although this book is nonfiction, it has all the elements of a novel: an exotic setting, in what was then British Africa (now Kenya); characters, both black and white, in whose lives and fortunes the reader becomes intensely involved; adventure; and a love story. The author recalls people, places, and events as she knew them as a child. We learn to know Tilly and Robin, her parents, who have come to Africa to raise coffee and hope to make their fortune; the Kikuyu and Masai who work for them; and their Scottish, Irish, English, and Dutch neighbors. The European and African cultures live side by side, each accepting, though seldom understanding, the strange ways of the other.

King, Martin Luther, Jr. *Stride Toward Freedom: The Montgomery Story*. (1958). New York and London: Harper & Row. 230 pp.

Available in paperback from Harper & Row, New York.

This is the dramatic story of what happened in Montgomery, Alabama when the Blacks decided to desegregate the buses on which they had been required to ride in the back. On December 1, 1955, Mrs. Rosa Parks, a black seamstress, refused to move to the back when her seat was needed for a white passenger. She was arrested. Her action inspired the other Blacks in Montgomery to boycott (refuse to ride) the buses. They were led in this peaceful protest by Dr. Martin Luther King Jr., an admirer of Gandhi and a believer in nonviolence. The boycott lasted over a year, and was finally resolved by a decision of the Supreme Court of the United States, which declared Alabama's segregation laws unconstitutional.
M

Laxalt, Robert. *Sweet Promised Land*. (1957). New York: Harper & Brothers. 176 pp.

The subject of this short biography is the author's father, Dominique, who left the Pyrenees Mountains as a young man and became a sheepherder in the western United States. When he was an old man, his children persuaded him to return to his birthplace to visit his Basque relatives. The trip serves as a framework for the book: the preparation; the trip to New York City; and finally, the father's trip to France and his reunion with his family. His life in America is described through conversations with his Basque relatives and friends.

Laye, Camara. *The Dark Child.* (1954). (J. Kirkup & E. Jones, Trans.). New York: Farrar, Strauss, & Giroux. (Original work published in 1953). 188 pp.

Available in paperback from Fontana, William Collins, London (titled *The African Child*); Farrar, Strauss & Giroux, New York.

The author of this autobiography tells of his childhood in French West Africa. His family life is happy. His father is wise and understanding; his mother is loving and protective; his uncles are kind and helpful; his aunts tease him gently about his girlfriend. He writes of visits to the country, of rituals which introduced him to young manhood, and finally of his departure to Paris for further study.

Lewis, C. S. *Letters to Children.* (1985). (L. W. Dorsett & M. L. Mead, Eds.). New York: Macmillan. 120 pp.

Lewis is a British author whose books of science fiction, fantasy, theology, and literary criticism are widely read. These letters begin in 1944 and end on November 21, 1963, the day before Lewis died. In them, Lewis answers questions that children have asked in their letters to him about his books, especially *The Chronicles of Narnia.* He shows an interest in the children's families, their schools, and their activities, and encourages them in their writing of stories and in their art and music.

The letters are carefully annotated, with allusions to literature explained. Young readers will probably not enjoy reading these letters as much as adults will, especially adults who have occasion to write letters to a child.

Liang Heng, & Shapiro, Judith. *Son of the Revolution.* (1983). New York: Alfred A. Knopf. London: Chatto & Windus. 300 pp.

Available in paperback from Random House, New York; Toronto; Fontana, London.

This autobiography begins with Liang Heng's experiences in nursery school, where he was "constantly in trouble for wanting to dance the army dance when it was time for the hoeing dance or for refusing to take the part of the landlord, the wolf, or the lazybones." It ends with his marriage to the American teacher who is his co-author.

The Liang family is affected by the frequent changes in the politcal situation in China, but the emphasis is on factional differences rather than on Communism as an ideology. The book describes the struggles of ordinary people trying to adjust to changes and at the same time remain loyal to their leaders and to their country.

M

(op) Lindbergh, Charles A. *"We"*. (1927). New York: G. P. Putnam's Sons. 318 pp.

The first nine chapters tell of Lindbergh's family, his early interest in flying, his stunt flying, his military training, and his flying the Air Mail. The pivotal chapter is the tenth, "New York to Paris." The book depicts a time when crossing an ocean by plane was unheard of, when planes often landed in roads or in cornfields, and pilots were not required to have a license. By flying from New York to Paris alone in a single-engine plane, Lindbergh became an international hero literally overnight. But as Fitzhugh Green, who wrote the last part of the book, points out, Lindbergh gave credit to others who had done aeronautical research, and the title of the book includes the people on both sides of the Atlantic who were with him in spirit on his flight.

Linderman, Frank. B. *Pretty-Shield: Medicine Woman of the Crows*. (1932). New York: John Day. Original title: *Red Mother*. New York: John Day. (op) 256 pp.

Available in paperback from University of Nebraska, Lincoln, NE; London.

The author interviewed Pretty-Shield, an elderly Crow Indian woman in Montana, communicating with her partly in sign language and partly with the aid of an interpreter. Most of Pretty-Shield's story is about her childhood on the plains. She tells tribal myths about creatures such as the ant-people and the antelope-people. She describes marriage customs, customs of war, and other aspects of American Indian life. Finally, she tells of the disappearance of the buffalo, killed by "the white man", and the effect of this disappearance on the Indians, who had depended on hunting buffalo for their livelihood.

Liu Zongren. *Ten Years in the Melting Pot.* (1984). San Francisco: China Books & Periodicals. 205 pp.

The author, a journalist, was sent by the Chinese government to study journalism in the United States. Most of his time was spent in Chicago, but he visited farms in the Midwest and attended the World's Fair in Knoxville, Tennessee. A keen observer, he gradually adjusted to American customs. He made many friends among various ethnic groups, including Chinese-Americans, Taiwanese, Filipinos, and American Blacks. This entertaining book is especially useful for anyone living in or planning to live in a foreign country.

Longgood, William. *The Queen Must Die: And Other Affairs of Bees and Men.* (1985). New York and London: W. W. Norton. 234 pp.

The author, who keeps bees as a hobby, seems more interested in observing their behavior and recording his observations than in giving advice to bee-keepers. He describes bee colonies in detail: the importance of the Queen and the ways in which she is cared for; the drones, who pursue the Queen on her "nuptial flight"; and the workers, daughters of the Queen, who feed her and care for her and then destroy her when she is no longer capable of laying enough eggs to satisfy the colony. The author frequently speculates on the behavior of bees and of men.
M

(op) Mikes, George. *Leap Through the Curtain: The Story of Nora Kovach and Istvan Robovsky.* (1956). New York: E. P. Dutton. 223 pp.

Nora and Istvan Rabovsky, ballet dancers, defected to the West by getting on an underground train in East Berlin. They had been treated well in both their native Hungary and Russia, and making up their minds to escape seemed more difficult for them than the actual deed. This book, written by George Mikes as it was dictated to him in Hungarian by Nora and Istvan, tells of their work as dancers in the Hungarian opera; of Istvan's poverty-stricken childhood; of Nora's strong ties to her mother; of the occupation of Budapest during World War II; of their fame and good fortune as dancers in the East. Their story is exciting and is told with frequent touches of humor; one need not have a particular interest in either ballet or politics to enjoy it.

(op) Miller, Maxine Adams. (As told by Ali Azizi). *Ali, a Persian Yankee*. (1965). Caldwell, Idaho: Caxton. 247 pp.

This autobiography recounts the adventures in the United States of an Iranian student who attended Queens College in New York, Indiana University, and the University of Southern California. When he arrived in New York he spoke very little English, and he had a number of awkward and often amusing experiences. In spite of his problems with language and customs he earned a graduate degree and returned to Iran. His friendship with Helen, a young American student who helped him with his English, adds interest to his story.

Moché, Dinah L. *Astronomy Today*. (1982). New York: Random House. London: Kingfisher. 96 pp.

This book explains why we have night and day, why the seasons change, the nature of starlight, the solar system, the importance of the sun, and the special nature of the planet Earth, the only planet that we know of which supports life. It describes telescopes and explains how they work. It discusses Russian as well as American space exploration, past and present, and considers future possiblities. It is packed with fascinating information, and is clearly and carefully written.
Y

Morison, Samuel Eliot. *Christopher Columbus, Mariner*. (1955). Boston: Little, Brown, & Co. (op) 260 pp.

Available in paperback from New American Library, New York; Scarborough, Ontario.

This account of the voyages and discoveries of Columbus is a shortened version of the two-volume edition entitled *Admiral of the Ocean Sea: A Life of Christopher Columbus*, published in 1942. The author emphasizes the superb seamanship, the firm religious faith, and the scientific curiosity of Columbus. He acknowledges that Columbus was not a successful colonizer, and that his several attempts to colonize the newly discovered lands ended in failure. Nor did Columbus ever understand that in attempting to find a new route to India, he had discovered lands which would become known as the New World.
M

Mowat, Farley. *Never Cry Wolf.* (1963). Boston: Little, Brown & Co. Toronto: McClelland & Stewart. 176 pp.

Available in paperback from Dell, New York; Seal, Toronto; Pan, London.

The author was sent by the Dominion Wildlife Service to study the habits of wolves in the Canadian wilderness. It was believed that they were destroying the caribou (large deer). He found that wolves eat only the sick or weak deer, and that this natural method of selection strengthens the species. Humans, on the other hand, try to kill the hardiest of the breed. He also found that wolves are peaceable animals with a highly developed social sense, living in families and caring for one another and for their young. The book also contains information about the wolves' diet, their mating habits, and their play.

Mphahlele, Ezekiel. *Down Second Avenue.* (1959). London: Faber & Faber. (op) Garden City, NY: Doubleday. (op)

Reprint edition available from Peter Smith, Magnolia, MA, and London. Available in paperback from Faber & Faber, Winchester, MA; London.

As a child the author lived in Marabastad, a South African ghetto. The first part of the book tells of his childhood, and of his struggle to get an education. He eventually became a teacher, and began to feel bitter toward the South African government becuase of its policies concerning the education of natives. Because he was courageously outspoken he was forbidden to teach and was forced to seek other employment. Eventually, with his wife and three children, he emigrated to Nigeria.

More a memoir than an autobiography, this book gives the reader insights into the effect of apartheid on South African Blacks.

Nkrumah, Kwame. *The Autobiography of Kwame Nkrumah.* (1957). (Published in the US as *Ghana: The Autobiography of Kwame Nkrumah.*). London: Thomas Nelson. New York: International Publishers. pp.

Available in paperback from Panaf, London; International Publishers, New York.

For most readers, the more interesting chapters in this book will be the early ones, in which the author describes his childhood in Africa and his studies in America and England. The remainder of the book is suitable for readers interested in the political, economic, and social problems that arise with the formation of a country, and the effectiveness of a strong leader in solving such problems. Nkrumah was such a leader. He traces his work in the formation of the government of Ghana, formerly known as the Gold Coast, from his preparatory days as a student to the final granting of the country's independence from Great Britain on March 6, 1957.
M

O'Connor, Karen. *Sally Ride and the New Astronauts: Scientists in Space*. (1983). New York, London, Toronto, and Sydney: Franklin Watts. 88 pp.

The emphasis is on Sally Ride, the first American woman in space, and other women astronauts. Related topics covered are specialists in space; preparations of astronauts; problems and how they have been solved; the phases of space shuttle missions; space centers; everyday life aboard a shuttle; and predictions for future space flights. It presents an excellent overall picture of space travel in this century.
Y

Orwell, George. *Homage to Catalonia*. (1938). London: Secker & Warburg. New York: Harcourt Brace. 232 pp.

Available in paperback from HarBrace, New York.

In 1937 Orwell went to Spain, where he joined the P.O.U.M. (*Partido Obrero de Univication Marxista*, a Marxist party) in order to fight against fascism. His report of the war is objective. The reader becomes aware of the often ridiculous, frequently pathetic, and sometimes tragic aspects of war, especially civil war. There is also confusion: The goals of the various political parties which banded together rather loosely in an unsuccessful attempt to defeat Franco are seldom clear, even to party members.

Students of modern history and students with a special interest in Spain will find this an enlightening book.
M

(op) Payne, Robert. *The Gold of Troy: The Story of Heinrich Schliemann and the Buried Cities of Ancient Greece.* (1959). New York: Funk & Wagnalls. 270 pp.

Schliemann has been called the founder of the modern science of archaeology. He believed that the city of Troy described by Homer was real, and eventually discovered and excavated ruins which seemed to be of that city.

The first part of this book tells of his early struggles. He was born poor but became wealthy through his diligence and talents. His incredible ability to learn languages (he mastered about a dozen) helped him greatly in business. After he had made several fortunes, he set out to excavate the Homeric city of Troy. The remainder of the book describes these excavations in detail.
M

Peare, Catherine Owens. *Mary McCloud Bethune.* (1951). New York: Vanguard. 219 pp.

Mary Jane McCloud was the 15th of 17 children born to former slaves Samuel and Patsy McCloud. After the slaves were freed in the United States, her parents managed to buy their own land, and with the help of their children they grew cotton. Mary's one interest in life was to be able to get an education and to teach. She did get her education, and eventually established a learning institute for black students in Daytona, Florida.

This book is a good introduction to the racial problems in the United States in the first half of this century. It describes the activities of the Ku Klux Klan; segregated facilities (drinking fountains, movie theaters, rest rooms, etc.); and other indignities that American Black citizens have endured.
Y

Peare, Catherine Owens. *The Helen Keller Story.* (1959). New York: Thomas Y. Crowell. Toronto: Fitzhenry & Whiteside. 188 pp.

Helen Keller was born in 1880 and became blind and deaf before she was 2 years old. When Helen was 7, Anne Sullivan came to the Keller home to care for her and teach her. Helen was a high-spirited, often difficult child, but eager to learn. Because of the skill and patience of Miss Sullivan, she learned to speak and eventually graduated from college with honors. As an adult she supported herself by writing books and magazine articles and by giving lectures. She became famous throughout the world.

This biography tells not only of her life and that of her teacher, but also of the progress made throughout the world in understanding and helping the deaf, the blind, and the deaf-blind.
Y

Pearlman, Moshe. *The Zealots of Masada: Story of a Dig.* (1967). New York: Charles Scribner's Sons. Paperback edition only. 210 pp.

In 1965 Professor Yigael Yadin led an archaeological expedition at the rock of Masada near the Dead Sea, where King Herod had built a palace in 30 B.C. A hundred years later, over 900 Zealots used Herod's buildings as a stronghold against the Roman army, and finally chose to die by their own hands rather than to surrender. The professor's expedition uncovered the ruins of Herod's time, of the Zealots, and of other peoples who had inhabited the rock. Members of the expedition included volunteers from 28 countries as well as trained archaeologists and technicians.
M

Shirer, William. *Gandhi: A Memoir.* (1979). New York: Simon & Schuster. 265 pp.

Available in paperback from Washington Square, New York.

The author is a noted journalist and author of nonfiction about political situations in various parts of the world. He met Mahatma Gandhi, whom he greatly admired, when he was 27 years old. In this memoir, Shirer emphasizes Gandhi's absolute honesty, his relentless determination to free India, his devotion to all humanity, and the loyalty of his followers. He also admits Gandhi's faults, and includes frank appraisals from those who did not think highly of Gandhi.
M

Siegal, Aranka. *Upon the Head of the Goat: A Childhood in Hungary, 1939-1944.* (1981). New York: Farrar, Strauss & Giroux. London: Dent. 215 pp.

This is the story of a Jewish family during World War II. Piri, as the author was called, was 9 years old in 1939. She lived with her mother, her grandmother, her sisters, her young stepbrother and stepsister, and her baby niece. Piri's stepfather and brother-in-law, both in the Hungarian army, could come home only occasionally for a visit. The women and children of this close and loving family struggled courageously to stay together and to help others who were being persecuted. The book ends when the five survivors get on a train which takes them to a concentration camp.
Y

Simon, Seymour. *The Secret Clocks: Time Senses of Living Things.* (1979). New York: Viking. Hormondsworth, Middlesex, England; Ringwood, Victoria, Australia; Markham, Ontario: Penguin. 66 pp.

This book discusses the ways in which many living things relate their behavior to a time schedule. Examples include the behavior of plants, the migration of birds; the feeding habits of animals in a zoo; the ways in which bees can be trained to come to a feeding station at a certain time; how the amount of oxygen used by a potato can predict the weather; and the sleep and activity rhythms of human beings. While external influences are considered, the emphasis is on the mystery of "internal clocks." The last chapter provides a number of simple experiments for the reader to perform.
Y

Solomon, Dorothy Allred. *In My Father's House.* (1984). New York and Toronto: Franklin Watts. 312 pp.

This autobiography describes the life of a Mormon family which practiced polygamy in 20th-century America, even though the laws of the nation and of their church forbade it. The author grew up with her father and mother, numerous brothers, six other wives of her father, and countless other relatives. There were happy times, but there were also problems: frequent moves to evade the law; the necessity to lie about their complex relationships; conflict with the Mormon Church; occasional friction among the wives; and the taunts of other children. In spite of the hardships, the author writes of her father with love rather than with resentment.
M

Steinbeck, John. *Travels with Charley: In Search of America*. (1962). New York: Viking. London: Heinemann. 245 pp.

Available in paperback from Bantam, New York; Pan, London.

The author, accompanied by his French poodle Charley, traveled across America's highways in his truck Rocinante (named for Don Quixote's horse). He reports fairly and entertainingly on all sections of the country: New England, the West, the South, and the Midwest. The book is a good description of the country as it was in 1962, and since Steinbeck deals with people and their attitudes rather than with politics and economics, it does not seem dated.

(op) Tenzing. (As told to James Ramsey Ullman). *Tiger of the Snows: The Autobiography of Tenzing of Everest*. (1955). New York: G. P. Putnam's Sons. 294 pp.

In this book Tenzing describes his youth in Nepal, his love of the mountains, and the work of his fellow Sherpas who serve as guides to mountain climbers. Tenzing became famous in 1953 when, accompanying Edmund Hillary of New Zealand, he reached the top of Everest, the highest mountain in the world. The emphasis throughout the book is on men facing danger and often death together, helping one another, and forming lasting friendships in spite of differences in nationality, race, culture, and language.

Though Tenzing became fluent in many languages, he was unable to read and write in any. The ghost writer, Ullman, maintains that Tenzing tells his own story in this book, however, in his own sincere way. For readers who wish to learn of his life and accomplishments in later years, another volume is available: *After Everest: An Autobiography*, by Tenzing Norgay, Sherpa, as told to Malcolm Barnes.

Terasaki, Gwen. *Bridge to the Sun*. (1957). Chapel Hill, NC, and London: University of North Carolina. Newport, TN: Wakestone. 260 pp.

The author was living in Washington D.C. with her husband Hidenari Terasaki and their 9-year-old daughter when the Japanese bombed Pearl Harbor in December 1941. She returned with her husband to Japan and lived there throughout the war and the American occupation. Even though the Japanese people were understanding and admired her for her bravery, she found living as an alien in a

country at war with her own a trying experience. This book depicts a little-known casualty of war: the plight of displaced nationals who choose to remain with their families in an enemy nation.
M

Vining, Elizabeth Gray. *Windows for the Crown Prince: An American Woman's Four Years as Private Tutor to the Crown Prince of Japan.* (1952). New York: Harper & Row. 320 pp.

At the end of World War II the author was employed by the Emperor of Japan to tutor the Crown Prince Akihito in English. Her duties included teaching in the schools attended by the Prince and other children. She stayed for 4 years, during which time the Prince and many of his classmates became proficient in the English language under her careful teaching. They also became familiar with American democratic ideals. Mrs. Vining became a close friend of the royal family, especially of the young prince, with whose character and poise she was greatly impressed.

Von Frisch, Karl. *Bees: Their Vision, Chemical Senses, and Languages.* (2nd ed.). (1971). Ithaca, NY: Cornell University. 109 pp.

Available in paperback from Cornell University, Ithaca, New York.

The author, an eminent zoologist, describes experiments he and his colleagues made to test the ability of bees to recognize colors and scents and to direct each other, by mean of their movements (described as a dance) to sources of food. No scientific background is needed to understand this clearly written book.

(op) Wong, Jade Snow. *Fifth Chinese Daughter.* (1945). New York: Harper & Brothers. 239 pp.

The author is a daughter in a Chinese immigrant family, with whom she lived in San Francisco. She writes of her schooling, both Chinese and American; her brothers and sisters; the tensions caused by cultural conflicts; her strict upbringing in the Chinese tradition; and the fulfillment of her desire to make her family proud of her. Weddings, parties, work habits, and customs in San Francisco's Chinese community are beautifully described. According to Chinese custom, this autobiography is related in the third person.

Appendices

Appendices

I. Cross Reference: Location

Africa: Fiction

    Achebe, C. *Things Fall Apart.* (Nigeria)
    Emecheta, B. *Second-Class Citizen.* (Nigeria)
    Lessing, D. *The Grass is Singing.* (South Africa)
    Paton, A. *Cry, the Beloved Country.* (South Africa)

Africa: Nonfiction

    Adamson, J. *Born Free.* (Kenya)
    Huxley, E. *The Flame Trees of Thika.* (Kenya)
    Laye, C. *The Dark Child.* (French West Africa)
    Mphalele, E. *Down Second Avenue.* (South Africa)
    Nkrumah, K. *Ghana: The Autobiography of Kwame Nkrumah.*

Asia, the Middle East, and the Pacific: Fiction

    Buck, P. *East Wind: West Wind.* (China)
    Gilman, D. *Mrs. Pollifax on the China Station.* (China)
    Godden, R. *The River.* (India)
    Hersey, J. *A Single Pebble.* (China)
    Ishiguro, K. *A Pale View of Hills.* (Japan)
    Jhabvala, R. P. *The Householder.* (India)
    Markandaya, K. *Nectar in a Sieve.* (India)
    Markandaya, K. *A Handful of Rice.* (India)
    Michener, J. *The Bridges at Toko-Ri.* (Korea)
    Narayan, R. K. *The English Teacher.* (India)
    Narayan, R. K. *A Tiger for Malgudi.* (India)
    Rachlin, N. *Foreigner.* (Iran)
    Rachlin, N. *Married to a Stranger.* (Iran)
    Shute, N. *A Town Like Alice.* (Malaysia and Australia)
    Wartski, M. C. *A Boat to Nowhere.* (Southeast Asia)
    Yep, L. *The Serpent's Children.* (China)

Asia, the Middle East, and the Pacific: Nonfiction

    Alireza, M. *At the Drop of a Veil.* (Arabia)
    Carter, J. *The Blood of Abraham: Insights into the Middle East.*
    Fritz, J. *Homesick: My Own Story.* (China)
    Fritz, J. *China Homecoming.* (China)
    Hersey, J. *Hiroshima.* (Japan)
    Liang Heng, & Shapiro, J. *Son of the Revolution.* (China)
    Miller, M. A. *Ali, a Persian Yankee.* (Iran)
    Pearlman, M. *The Zealots of Masada.* (Middle East)
    Shirer, W. L. *Gandhi.* (India)
    Tenzing. *Tiger of the Snows.* (Nepal)
    Terasaki, G. *Bridge to the Sun.* (Japan)
    Vining, E. G. *Windows for the Crown Prince.* (Japan)

Canada and the United States: Fiction

    Aldrich, B. S. *A Lantern in Her Hand.* (US: Nebraska)
    Anaya, R. *Bless Me, Ultima.* (US: Southwest)
    Burnford, S. *The Incredible Journey.* (Canada)
    Cather, W. *O Pioneers!* (US: Nebraska)
    Cleaver, V., & Cleaver, B. *Where the Lilies Bloom.* (US: Great Smoky Mountains)
    Craven, M. *I Heard the Owl Call My Name.* (Canada: British Columbia)
    Forbes, K. *Mama's Bank Account.* (US: San Francisco)
    Fritz, J. *Brady.* (US)
    George, J. C. *Julie of the Wolves.* (US: Alaska)
    Gilman, D. *A Nun in the Closet.* (US: New York)
    Kemelman, H. *Friday the Rabbi Slept Late.* (US: Massachusetts)
    Knowles, J. *A Separate Peace.* (US: New Hampshire)
    L'Engle, M. *Meet the Austins.* (US: New England)
    Moberg, V. *Unto a Good Land.* (US: Minnesota)
    Richter, C. *The Light in the Forest.* (US: Pennsylvania)
    Schaefer, J. *Shane.* (US: West)
    Tyler, A. *Dinner at the Homesick Restaurant.* (US: Southeast)
    Uchida, Y. *Journey Home.* (US: California)
    Voight, C. *Homecoming.* (US: East)
    Wartski, M. C. *A Long Way from Home.* (US: California)
    Waters, F. *The Man Who Killed the Deer.* (US: Southwest)
    White, E. B. *Charlotte's Web.* (US)
    Wibberley, L. *The Mouse That Roared.* (US: New York)
    Yep, L. *Dragonwings.* (US: California)

Canada and the United States: Nonfiction

    Anonymous. *Go Ask Alice*. (US)
    Baker, R. *Growing Up*. (US: Virginia)
    Boeri, D. *People of the Ice Whale*. (US: Alaska)
    Deford, F. *Alex: The Life of a Child*. (US: New England)
    Gilbreth, F. B., Jr., & Carey, E. G. *Cheaper by the Dozen*. (US)
    Gruber, R. *Felisa Rincón de Gautier* (US: Puerto Rico)
    Hareven, T. *Eleanor Roosevelt*. (US)
    King, M. L., Jr. *Stride Toward Freedom*. (US: Alabama)
    Lindbergh, C. A. *"We"*. (US)
    Linderman, F. B. *Pretty Shield: Medicine Woman of the Crows*. (US: Montana)
    Liu Zongren. *Ten Years in the Melting Pot*. (US)
    Miller, M. A. *Ali, a Persian Yankee*. (US)
    Mowat, F. *Never Cry Wolf*. (Canada)
    Peare, C. O. *Mary McCloud Bethune*. (US: the South)
    Peare, C. O. *The Helen Keller Story*. (US: Alabama)
    Solomon, D. A. *In My Father's House*. (US: the West)
    Steinbeck, J. *Travels with Charley*. (US)
    Wong, J. S. *Fifth Chinese Daughter*. (US: San Francisco)

Europe: Fiction

    Burnett, F. H. *The Secret Garden*. (England)
    Christie, A. *Crooked House*. (England)
    Emecheta, B. *Second-Class Citizen*. (London)
    Godden, R. *The Diddakoi*. (England)
    Harris, R. *Zed*. (London)
    Hersey, J. *A Bell for Adano*. (Italy)
    Ishiguro, K. *A Pale View of Hills*. (England)
    Remarque, E. M. *All Quiet on the Western Front*. (Germany)
    Sarton, M. *Joanna and Ulysses*. (Greece)
    Steinbeck, J. *The Short Reign of Pippin IV*. (France)
    Stewart, M. *The Moon-Spinners*. (Crete)

Europe: Nonfiction

    Cavanah, F. *Jenny Lind and Her Listening Cat*. (Sweden)
    Frank, A. *Anne Frank: The Diary of a Young Girl*. (The Netherlands)
    Hautzig, E. *The Endless Steppe: Growing Up in Siberia*. (Poland, Russia)

Laxalt, R. *Sweet Promised Land.* (French Pyrenees)
Lewis, C. S. *Letters to Children.* (England)
Mikes, G. *Leap Through the Curtain.* (Hungary, Germany, Russia)
Orwell, G. *Homage to Catalonia.* (Spain)
Payne, R. *The Gold of Troy.* (Greece)
Siegal, A. *Upon the Head of the Goat.* (Hungary)

Latin America: Fiction

Greene, G. *Our Man in Havana.* (Cuba)
Hemingway, E. *The Old Man and the Sea.* (Caribbean)
O'Dell, S. *The Black Pearl.* (Mexico)
O'Dell, S. *The Captive.* (Mexico)
Saint Exupéry, A. de. *Night Flight.* (South America)
Steinbeck, J. *The Pearl.* (Mexico)
Wilder, T. *The Bridge of San Luis Rey.* (Peru)

Latin America: Nonfiction

Gruber, R. *Felisa Rincón de Gautier.* (Puerto Rico)
Morison, S. E. *Christopher Columbus, Mariner* (Caribbean)

United States (See Canada and the United States)

II. Cross Reference: Topics and *Genres* (Literary Types)

Animals: Fiction

    Burnford, S. *The Incredible Journey.*
    George, J. C. *Julie of the Wolves.*
    Lewis, C. S. *The Lion, the Witch and the Wardrobe.*
    Narayan, R. K. *A Tiger for Malgudi.*
    Sarton, M. *Joanna and Ulysses.*
    White, E. B. *Charlotte's Web.*

Animals: Nonfiction

    Adamson, J. *Born Free.*
    Boeri, D. *People of the Ice Whale.*
    Longgood, W. *The Queen Must Die.*
    Mowat, F. *Never Cry Wolf.*
    Von Frisch, K. *Bees: Their Vision, Chemical Sense, and Languages.*

Autobiography, Biography, Diaries, Letters, Memoirs

    Anonymous. *Go Ask Alice.*
    Baker, R. *Growing Up.*
    Bernstein, J. *Einstein.*
    Cavanah, F. *Jenny Lind and Her Listening Cat.*
    Deford, F. *Alex: The Life of a Child.*
    Frank, A. *Anne Frank: Diary of a Young Girl.*
    Fritz, J. *Homesick: My Own Story.*
    Fritz, J. *China Homecoming.*
    Gilbreth, F., Jr., & Carey, E. G. *Cheaper by the Dozen.*
    Gruber, R. *Felisa Rincón de Gautier.*
    Hareven, T. K. *Eleanor Roosevelt: An American Conscience.*
    Hautzig, E. *The Endless Steppe.*
    Huxley, E. *The Flame Trees of Thika.*
    King, M. L., Jr. *Stride Toward Freedom: The Montgomery Story.*
    Laye, C. *The Dark Child.*
    Lewis, C. S. *Letters to Children.*
    Liang Heng, & Shapiro, J. *Son of the Revolution.*
    Lindbergh, C. A. *"We".*
    Liu Zongren. *Ten Years in the Melting Pot.*
    Mikes, G. *Leap Through the Curtain.*

Miller, M. A. *Ali, a Persian Yankee.*
Morison, S. E. *Christopher Columbus, Mariner.*
Mphahlele, E. *Down Second Avenue: Growing Up in a South African Ghetto.*
Nkrumah, K. *Ghana: The Autobiography of Kwame Nkrumah.*
Payne, R. *The Gold of Troy.*
Peare, C. O. *Mary McCloud Bethune.*
Peare, C. O. *The Helen Keller Story.*
Shirer, W. L. *Gandhi: A Memoir.*
Siegal, A. *Upon the Head of the Goat.*
Solomon, D. A. *In My Father's House.*
Tenzing. *Tiger of the Snows.*
Wong, J. S. *Fifth Chinese Daughter.*

Mystery and Espionage

Christie, A. *Crooked House.*
Gilman, D. *A Nun in the Closet.*
Gilman, D. *Mrs. Pollifax on the China Station.*
Greene, G. *Our Man in Havana.*
Kemelman, H. *Friday the Rabbi Slept Late.*

Native Americans, Eskimos, Chicanos: Fiction

Anaya, R. *Bless Me, Ultima.*
Craven, M. *I Heard the Owl Call My Name.*
George, J. C. *Julie of the Wolves.*
Richter, C. *The Light in the Forest.*
Waters, F. *The Man Who Killed the Deer.*

Native Americans, Eskimos: Nonfiction

Boeri, D. *People of the Ice Whale.*
Linderman, F. B. *Pretty Shield: Medicine Woman of the Crows.*
Mowat, F. *Never Cry Wolf.*

Science

Asimov, I. *How Did We Find Out About Outer Space?* (physics)
Bernstein, J. *Einstein.* (physics)
Clarke, A. C. *Exploration of Space.* (physics)
Collins, M. *Flying to the Moon and Other Strange Places.*

Lindbergh, C. A. *"We"*. (aviation)
Longgood, W. *The Queen Must Die*. (biology)
Moché, D. L. *Astronomy Today*.
Mowat, F. *Never Cry Wolf*. (biology)
O'Connor, K. *Sally Ride and the New Astronauts: Scientists in Space*.
Payne, R. *The Gold of Troy*. (archaeology)
Pearlman, M. *The Zealots of Masada*. (archaeology)
Simon, S. *The Secret Clocks: Time Senses of Living Things*. (biology)
Von Frisch, K. *Bees: Their Vision, Chemical Sense, and Languages*. (biology)

Science Fiction and Fantasy

Adams, D. *The Hitchhiker's Guide to the Galaxy*.
Bradbury, R. *Fahrenheit 451*.
Lewis, C. S. *Out of the Silent Planet*.
Lewis, C. S. *The Lion, the Witch, and the Wardrobe*.
Saint Exupéry, A. de. *The Little Prince*.

Visitors, Immigrants, Refugees, Explorers: Fiction

Emecheta, B. *Second-Class Citizen*. (Nigerians in London)
Forbes, K. *Mama's Bank Account*. (Norwegians in San Francisco)
Gilman, D. *Mrs. Pollifax on the China Station*. (Americans in China)
Greene, G. *Our Man in Havana*. (British in Cuba)
Hersey, J. *A Bell for Adano*. (Americans in Italy)
Hersey, J. *A Single Pebble*. (Americans in China)
Ishiguro, K. *A Pale View of Hills*. (Japanese in England)
Lessing, D. *The Grass is Singing*. (British in South Africa)
Moberg, V. *Unto a Good Land*. (Swedes in the US)
Rachlin, N. *Foreigner*. (Iranian returns home after living in the US)
Shute, N. *A Town Like Alice*. (Londoner in Malaysia and Australia)
Stewart, M. *The Moon-Spinners*. (British in Greece)
Wartski, M. C. *A Long Way From Home*. (Vietnamese in California)
Yep, L. *Dragonwings*. (Chinese in San Francisco)

Visitors, Immigrants, Refugees, Explorers: Nonfiction

Adamson, J. *Born Free.* (English in Kenya)
Alireza, M. *At the Drop of a Veil.* (American in Arabia)
Fritz, J. *Homesick: My Own Story.* (Americans in China)
Fritz, J. *China Homecoming.* (Americans in China)
Huxley, E. *The Flame Trees of Thika.* (British in Kenya)
Laxalt, R. *Sweet Promised Land.* (French Basques in the US; Americans in the French Pyrenees)
Liu Zongren. *Ten Years in the Melting Pot.* (Chinese in the US)
Miller, M. A. *Ali, a Persian Yankee.* (Iranian in the US)
Morison, S. E. *Christopher Columbus, Mariner.* (Spaniards in the Carribbean)
Orwell, G. *Homage to Catalonia.* (American in Spain)
Terasaki, G. *Bridge to the Sun.* (American in Japan)
Vining, E. G. *Windows for the Crown Prince.* (Americans in Japan)
Wong, J. S. *Fifth Chinese Daughter.* (Chinese in San Francisco)

War and Peace: Fiction

Fritz, J. *Brady.* (US Civil War)
Hersey, J. *A Bell for Adano.* (World War II)
Knowles, J. *A Separate Peace.* (World War II)
Michener, J. *The Bridges at Toko-Ri.* (Korean War)
Remarque, E. M. *All Quiet on the Western Front.* (World War I)
Shute, N. *A Town Like Alice.* (World War II)
Uchida, Y. *Journey Home.* (World War II)
Wartski, M. C. *A Boat to Nowhere.* (Vietnamese War)
Wartski, M. C. *A Long Way From Home.* (Vietnamese War)
Wibberley, L. *The Mouse That Roared.* (Satire on war)

War and Peace: Nonfiction

Frank, A. *Anne Frank: Diary of a Young Girl.* (World War II)
Hautzig, E. *The Endless Steppe.* (World War II)
Hersey, J. *Hiroshima.* (World War II)
Liang Heng & Shapiro, J. *Son of the Revolution.* (Chinese revolution)
Orwell, G. *Homage to Catalonia.* (Spanish Civil War)
Siegal, A. *Upon the Head of the Goat.* (World War II)
Terasaki, G. *Bridge to the Sun.* (World War (II)
Vining, E. G. *Windows for the Crown Prince.* (World War II)

III. Some Short and Easy Books

Fiction

    Burnford, S. *The Incredible Journey.*
    Cleaver, V., & Cleaver, B. *Where the Lilies Bloom.*
    Forbes, K. *Mama's Bank Account.*
    George, J. C. *Julie of the Wolves.*
    Godden, R. *The River.*
    Godden, R. *The Diddakoi.*
    Harris, R. *Zed.*
    Hemingway, E. *The Old Man and the Sea.*
    L'Engle, M. *Meet the Austins.*
    Lewis, C. S. *The Lion, the Witch, and the Wardrobe.*
    O'Dell, S. *The Black Pearl.*
    Richter, C. *The Light in the Forest.*
    Saint Exupéry, A. de. *The Little Prince.*
    Sarton, M. *Joanna and Ulysses.*
    Schaeffer, J. *Shane.*
    Steinbeck, J. *The Pearl.*
    Uchida, Y. *Journey Home.*
    Wartski, M. C. *A Boat to Nowhere.*
    Wartski, M. C. *A Long Way From Home.*
    White, E. B. *Charlotte's Web.*

Nonfiction

    Asimov, I. *How Did We Find Out About Outer Space?*
    Cavanah, F. *Jenny Lind and Her Listening Cat.*
    Collins, M. *Flying to the Moon and Other Strange Places.*
    Fritz, J. *China Homecoming.*
    Fritz, J. *Homesick: My Own Story.*
    Gruber, R. *Felisa Rincón de Gautier: Mayor of San Juan.*
    Hersey, J. *Hiroshima.*
    Laye, C. *The Dark Child.*
    Lewis, C. S. *Letters to Children.*
    Liu Zongren. *Ten Years in the Melting Pot.*
    Moché, D. L. *Astronomy Today.*
    Mowat, F. *Never Cry Wolf.*
    O'Connor, K. *Sally Ride and the New Astronauts: Scientists in Space.*
    Peare, C. O. *Mary McCloud Bethune.*
    Peare, C. O. *The Helen Keller Story.*
    Siegal, A. *Upon the Head of the Goat.*
    Simon, S. *The Secret Clocks: Time Senses of Living Things.*
    Wong, J. S. *Fifth Chinese Daughter.*

IV. For Advanced Readers

Fiction

    Adams, D. *The Hitchhiker's Guide to the Galaxy.*
    Bradbury, R. *Fahrenheit 451.*
    Hersey, J. *A Single Pebble.*
    Ishiguro, K. *A Pale View of Hills.*
    Knowles, J. *A Separate Peace.*
    Lessing, D. *The Grass is Singing.*
    Tyler, A. *Dinner at the Homesick Restaurant.*

Nonfiction

    Clarke, A. C. *The Exploration of Space.*
    Hareven, T. K. *Eleanor Roosevelt: An American Conscience.*
    Longgood, W. *The Queen Must Die.*
    Morison, S. *Christopher Columbus, Mariner.*
    Orwell, G. *Homage to Catalonia.*
    Shirer, W. *Gandhi: A Memoir.*